Demystifying SNA

Ed Taylor

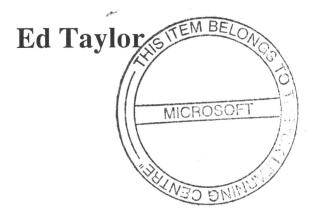

THIS ITEM BELONGS TO THE LEARNING CENTRE

MICROSOFT

Wordware Publishing, Inc.

C.2 4.1
SNA
TAY

Library of Congress Cataloging-in-Publication Data

Taylor, Ed, 1958-
    Demystifying SNA / by Ed Taylor.
      p. cm.
    Includes index.
    ISBN 1-55622-404-4
    1. SNA (Computer network architecture).   I. Title.
    TK5105.5.T39   1993
    004.6--dc20   93-32524
                                                     CIP

ISBN 1-55622-404-4

10 9 8 7 6 5 4 3 2 1

9308

All product names mentioned are used for identification purposes only and may be trademarks of
their respective companies.

All inquiries for volume purchases of this book should be addressed to
Wordware Publishing, Inc., at the above address. Telephone inquiries may be
made by calling:

(214) 423-0090

Contents

Acknowledgements

In their own way, these individuals have contributed much to my life.

Zac

Ted

Mindy May

Trudy Gandy

George Wynne

O. E. Perry

Wanda Greer

Sonny May

Ginny Brown

William Howard

Silver Star Cleaners

Don Davis

John Gandy

Luther Adkins

MONT BLANC

Tumi

Bill Lathum

Jim Woodward

Johnny Walton

Dr. Samuel L. Gladney

Ceil Perry

Audrey Talbott

Robert Talbott in Carmel

Jerry Perry

Dee

Frances Tucker

D. N. Matthews

Raleigh Cutrer

Charles E. Bailey

Zelma Gandy (call me if you have any problems reading dumps)

Dedicated To:

Zac

Ted

Cynthia Fetty

4ED

Preface

Systems Network Architecture (SNA) is a complex topic. This book explains certain terms and concepts at the heart of SNA. The book is especially suited for those just beginning to work with SNA and/or APPN. It is designed to be a starting point for those not knowing how to tackle the topic of SNA. If you read it straight through as I intended it to be, you will be considereably more knowledgeable about SNA.

Chapter 1 explains how to begin learning SNA. It explains some of the hardware and software SNA is based upon.

Chapter 2 examines software components in SNA. This includes communication software and applications.

Chapter 3 presents common terms and concepts in SNA. They are explained and clear definitions are used.

Chapter 4 orients the reader to the evolution of SNA. It was placed after chapter 3 because certain terms and concepts are required to take advantage of this information.

Chapter 5 explains VTAM in light of its function in SNA. Certain VTAM components are presented and defined.

Chapter 6 explores APPN. This information is pertinent to SNA because the two arenas are becoming closly intertwined.

Chapter 1

How to Learn SNA

The most difficult thing about Systems Network Architecture (SNA) is how to learn it. This chapter focuses upon how to tackle the problem of learning SNA. By learn, I mean understand SNA. This book does not emphasize *memorizing*, but understanding. If one truly understands SNA, memorization of the details will occur by default. This chapter presents much of the hardware components that make up SNA, and some of the software is presented, specifically operating systems. Understanding these pieces is important before examining abstract topics that will come later. Bear in mind to focus upon the big picture, while not losing sight of the pieces.

1.1 Understanding Basic Facts About SNA

A good way to approach SNA is by accepting some facts about it. For example, some general facts about SNA include the following:

- IBM created it.
- IBM controls its direction, refinement, and evolution.
- It is one of the largest and most widespread networking protocols in existence today.
- SNA is built upon hardware and software architectures.
- SNA components include specific hardware and software. These components are built upon the architectures defined by IBM.
- SNA consists of its own terms and concepts that IBM created and defined.

- A considerable amount of SNA is abstract, and learning it is difficult.
- Learning SNA is a catch 22 situation. One cannot understand its concepts without understanding the terms they are based upon. But, understanding SNA terms requires basic understanding of some concepts.
- SNA is a protocol. This means there is a defined way of doing things within an SNA network. Operations work a certain way. They have a predefined structure.
- Because of the SNA structure, benefits and limitations result.

1.2   Bringing the Abstract into Reality

Understanding SNA is tricky. Since IBM literally created the "wheel," they wrote the book including hardware and software components, terms, and concepts. For some, it is difficult to learn because of its structure, but this structure makes learning it easy for others. SNA is based on hardware and software components, and consequently, it can be analyzed from a hardware and a software perspective.

1.3   A Perspective on Hardware

IBM's hardware architectural lineage is traceable and clearly definable. IBM's first big gamble, according to popular opinion, was the System 360 (S/360) architecture announced in 1964. This announcement was considered a gamble of significant proportions because IBM was attempting to bring together different systems that had been designed to perform specific tasks. IBM's goal was to put these diverse systems under one architectural umbrella.

In the 1950s IBM became increasingly aware of strains placed on the company because of its endeavor to support different technologies resulting in diverse computer systems. For example, IBM's efforts in the 1940s and 1950s produced systems (product lines and different models) such as the following:

- 701—Focused on raw calculating speed.
- 702—Emphasized ease of handling characters.

- 650—Offered comparatively low costs and focused on general computations.
- 1401—Offered multiple components making it an attractive choice for those needing card readers, printers, the processing unit, tape units, and disk drives.
- 604—This was an electronic calculating punch card system and was considered to be a high speed machine.

IBM had other systems during the 1940s and 1950s, but the point is, IBM realized it was spread thin and began to focus upon developing a single system. The goal of a single system was to meet a variety of needs and provide a growth pattern for customers so migration from one system size to the next would have nominal impact. Compared to IBM's diverse systems this new approach was revolutionary. Herein was the impetus for a single hardware architecture.

The Turning Point

The S/360 architecture was envisioned to be the vehicle customers could use to minimize expenditure while maximizing results. This architecture provided the means for upgrading processors to a more powerful model with nominal impact on programs and related areas impacting expenditure and day-to-day business operations. A quick review of IBM's architecture and related timetable provides insight to the architectural growth IBM has provided its customers since 1964.

Hardware Architecture Timetable

The hardware architectural lineage and associated time frames include:

- S/360   1964
- S/370   1971
- 370/XA   1981
- 370/ESA   1988
- S/390   1990

1.4 Hardware Architecture

A summary of hardware architecture provides enough insight to the evolution in technology through the past 28 years. For example, the S/360 was the first break with IBM's past that supported multiple architectures. The S/360 provided a single architectural line providing growth potential with little disruption, a wide range of supporting peripheral equipment, and consolidation of IBM's internal efforts to support one architecture. In short, it was IBM's effort to leverage the power of synergy. Figure 1.1 depicts the S/360 architecture.

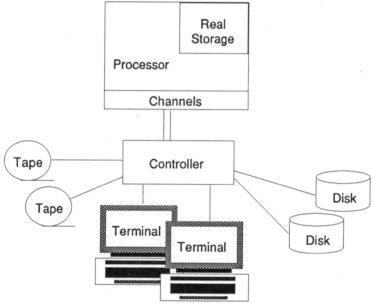

Figure 1.1   S/360 Architecture

Figure 1.1 shows a processor; it executes programs. Processors also have storage (some refer to this as memory). Channels are electronic devices that data must pass across en route to the processor. The controller is a device to which tape drives, disks, terminals, and printers can be attached. Its basic function is coordination of communication of these devices with the processor.

The next architecture was the S/370. It was designed with the following features and functions:

- Virtual storage. This provided a different way of manipulating data. It added power to the processing process.

- Dual processor support increased the processing capability. This was the next step in the architectural evolution. The S/360 primarily supported a single processor.

- 24 bit addressing. This permitted the processor to handle more memory than the S/360.

- An expanded instruction set beyond the S/360 providing enhanced program flexibility.

- Support for three types of channels (data paths) into the processor were supported. They were:

  - selector
  - byte
  - block multiplexer

All data inbound to a processor goes across a channel. The term channel is used generically to refer to a path. In IBM terminology it has specific meaning. It refers to a type of path reflecting how data is transferred to the processor. Figure 1.2 shows how the different channels appear conceptually in this architecture.

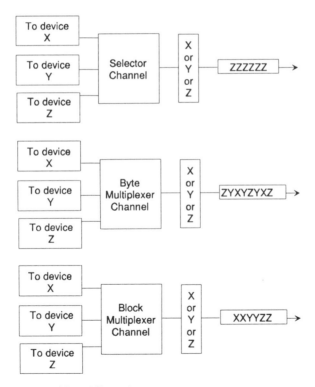

Figure 1.2 Conceptual View of Channels

What figure 1.2 shows is how data is handled differently with different channel types. For example, the selector channel will permit data transfer from either device X, Y, or Z. The channel "selects" which device will transmit data across it. This type channel operated whereby one device at a time transmitted data.

The byte multiplexer channel has the capability to multiplex (interweave) data from different devices, such as device X, Y, or Z. This type channel permits data transfer in bytes from transmitting devices.

The block multiplexer channel handled data similar to the byte multiplexer channel, with the exception that it allowed data transmission in blocks. Hence, blocks of data from varying devices could be multiplexed together thereby maximizing channel bandwidth.

- The concept of channel ownership by the CPU. This meant in a dual processor system a given processor could own a channel, thus enhancing performance. This concept of ownership provides maximum flexibility and load balancing.
- Maximum real storage (memory) amount was 16 Mb.

Figure 1.3 depicts the S/370 architecture.

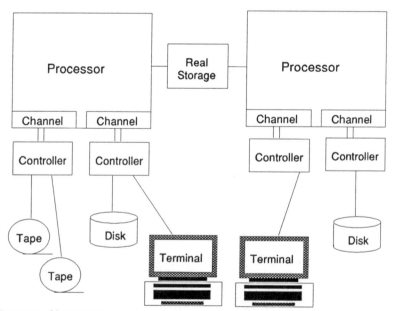

Figure 1.3   S/370 Architecture

Figure 1.3 depicts two processors sharing real storage. Each processor owns channels. Resource sharing between the two processor complexes is achievable.

IBM's 370/XA followed S/370 architecture. It added functionality including:

- A distinct channel I/O subsystem. Previous architectures had the channel subsystem built into the processor component packaging.
- Channels were not owned by a particular CPU. This permitted flexibility among the processors so they could work together.
- A 31 bit addressing scheme was used, thus more memory could be supported.
- Maximum storage (memory) amount was 2 gigabytes.
- This architecture supported both S/370 mode (24 bit addressing) and/or XA mode (31 bit addressing). This meant XA architecture was backward compatible.

Figure 1.4 depicts the 370/XA architecture.

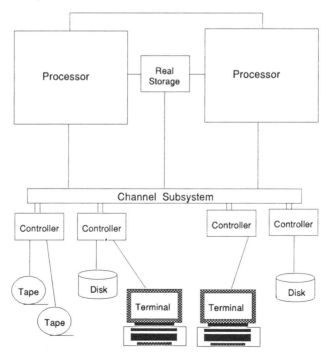

Figure 1.4   370/XA Architecture

Figure 1.4 shows a channel subsystem, independent from the processor complex. A cache (memory that operates very fast) was implemented in the subsystem, thus enhancing performance. The channel subsystem provided a dynamic channel ownership for CPUs permitting maximum flexibility for processor operation.

A 31 bit addressing scheme was used. This increased the amount of supported memory to 2 gigabytes. Because of its design it was backward compatible and could run programs written for processors using the 24 bit addressing scheme.

370/ESA followed the XA architecture. Basic characteristics of 370/ESA include the following:

- A storage hierarchy where data is staged in the following order:
  - Central Processing Unit (CPU)
  - CPU cache
  - central storage (main storage)
  - expanded storage
  - Direct Access Storage Device (DASD) cache
  - DASD
  - tape or other means of archiving

This concept of staging data in respect to storage increased the overall processing time. Figure 1.5 depicts this storage hierarchy.

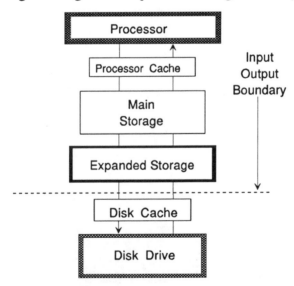

Figure 1.5   Storage Hierarchy

Figure 1.5 depicts the I/O boundary that is significant because of how data was managed. With the help of other offerings made with ESA/370, data could now be moved up and down the hierarchy of storage. Thus the concept of system managed storage was introduced.

- The System Control Element (SCE) is responsible for routing data throughout the hierarchy. It was also responsible for managing data in the storage hierarchy.

- The Data Facility Storage Management Subsystem (DFSMS), a collection of software programs used to provide a user friendly interface for storage management, was introduced. It brought together different program offerings and made storage management more dynamic, meaning the system was more in control of data storage.

- It supported 16 terabytes of addressing capability. This meant expanded capabilities with regard to production capacity.

- A linking program function was built into the hardware providing automatic stack and unstack functions. This linking function contributed to overall increased speed.

Figure 1.6 is a basic representation of 370/ESA architecture.

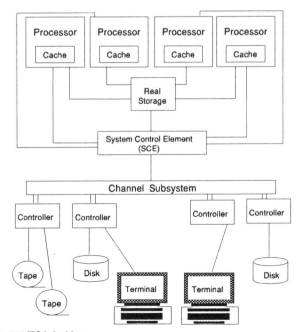

Figure 1.6   370/ESA Architecture

370/ESA supported 16 terabytes of memory. The Data Facility Storage Management Subsystem (DFSMS) is comprised of numerous software products. From a storage management standpoint, IBM brought these packages together, making them the focal point in the storage hierarchy.

Other features of ESA/370 included:

- Moving data between two address spaces
- Passing control between address spaces

S/390 followed ESA/370 architecture. Highlights of it include:

- An initial line of 26 processor models either air or water cooled. They are known as the ES/9000 Series. These machines support functions that mainframes of other architectures did not.

- A major addition to the S/390 was the change in the I/O subsystem. With the S/390 came Enterprise System Connectivity (ESCON); simply put, IBM's fiber optic I/O system. The fiber subsystem replaces the channels of prior architectures. ESCON channels operate serially and provide significant throughput capability as well as supporting longer physical distances than channels of previous architectures. These previous channels are still around; they have been renamed as parallel channels.

- Another addition with the S/390 was the 3172 Interconnect controller. Its strength is support for various LAN implementations. This addition brought support for a variety of LANs. It has since been the focal point for the TCP/IP offload feature.

- An enhanced version of VTAM supporting LAN implementations and remote system links was also part of the S/390 architecture offering.

- System View was introduced. It is an enhanced method of system management and a new system management product design structure.

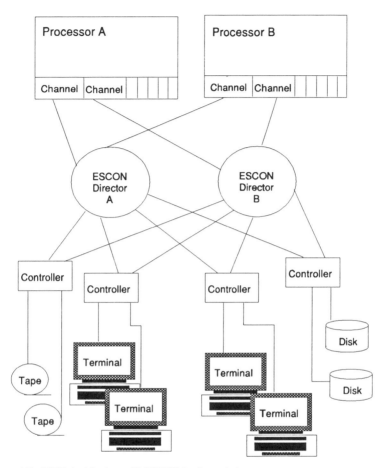

Figure 1.7   S/390 Architecture with ESCON Implemented

Figure 1.7 is one example of an S/390 implementation. It shows the ESCON directors and ESCON channels. This was the significant announcement with the S/390 architecture. IBM re-engineered the I/O subsystem. The prior subsystem (with channels) was renamed as parallel channels. ESCON transmits data serially, but at higher speeds and greater distances than parallel channels.

Other announcements accompanied the S/390 offering. These are but a few. As a combined package, the scope of this offering affected the largest part of IBM's product line. Most of the announcements related to S/390 built upon prior architectures.

Over the past decades, each successive generation of architecture brought new features, functions, and products (typically hardware and software). The idea driving this approach was to maintain a common thread through different generations of architecture. By doing this, the link to make the next architectural leap without totally re-creating programs, data, etc was achieved. Each architectural generation has taken advantage of state-of-the-art technology and brought it to the marketplace in a useable fashion, while supporting its forerunner.

1.5 Breaking the Number Barrier

Processors

Many times confusion arises over numbers used in conversations about SNA hardware architecture/components. Deciphering these numbers is easy if one understands the structure. The following example uses processors to explain the numbering system used by IBM.

Processors are based on an architecture. The most popular architectures are:

- S/370
- 370/XA
- 370/ESA
- S/390

Processors are also categorized by series; for example:

- 4300
- 9300
- 3090

Each of the series have models. For example, the 4300 series of processors have approximately a dozen individual models. An example of two models in the 4300 series are:

- Model 4341
- Model 4381

Another example from the 3090 series would be the following models:

- Model J
- Model S

Numbers have meaning. Knowing the architecture, processor series, and models is enough information to deduce additional information such as the processing capabilities of that processor. Figure 1.8 depicts an ES/9000 processor.

Figure 1.8 ES/9000 Processor

Ironically, as processors become more powerful, they are becoming smaller.

3174 Establishment Controller

This device succeeds the 3274 cluster controller. Both the 3174 and 3274 are devices to which 3270 type terminals and printers attach. Consequently, the 3174 is an integral part of the 3270 Information Display System. The 3174 consists of different models, each having special offerings/features providing a range of products. Fundamentally, the 3174 is a communications processor with models supporting network management functions, a variety of physical layer connecting interfaces, 3270 data stream support, and other SNA related functions. Figure 1.9 depicts a processor and a 3174 Establishment Controller.

Figure 1.9 3174 Establishment Controller

Terminals

IBM's large systems are primarily based on what is called a 3270 data stream. This is a format and protocol used with most large IBM processors. The data stream was designed and embedded into architectures years ago. Consequently, 3270 type terminals exist. Actually, the number 3270 indicates an entire family of devices built around the specifications accommodating the 3270 data stream.

Other data streams exist, but the 3270 data stream is dominant. An example of a 3270 type terminal could be the 3278. This type terminal has 4 models, differing in characteristics. They include:

- model 2
- model 3
- model 4
- model 5

Each of these have specific characteristics, but they differ in the number of columns and rows supported. However, they all have the 3270 data stream in common.

Other numbers reflecting terminals exist such as the 3179G. This is a graphics terminal, but it too operates on a 3270 data stream. Figure 1.10 depicts a processor, 3174, and terminals.

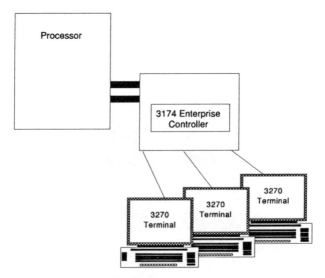

Figure 1.10   Processor, 3174 and Terminals

Printers

IBM offers a variety of printers for its large processors. Some printer types include: line, thermal, laser, band, and others. Normally, these are integrated via a controller of some type. Different numbers are associated with printer types. Printers do not necessarily follow a particular series or family order. They do however support different software data streams. Figure 1.11 depicts a processor, 3174, terminals, and printers.

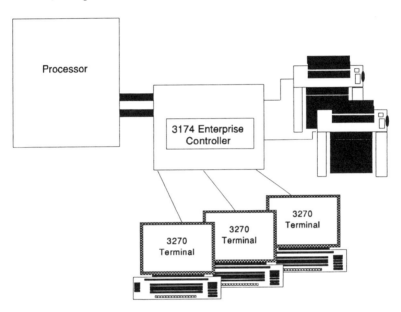

Figure 1.11   Processor, 3174, Terminals, and Printers

3720 and 3745 Communication Controllers

These devices, also known as front-end processors (FEPs), support data link protocols like SDLC, Token Ring, Parallel Channel, and others. The model dictates the capabilities of the device. Both use a Network Control Program (NCP) and support other programs providing additional functionality. These devices support a significant amount of work load themselves; hence, they are referred to as front-end processors. Figure 1.12 depicts a processor and a 3745 including a NCP.

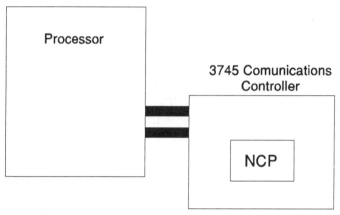

Figure 1.12   Processor and 3745

The communications controller is typically how SNA networks are connected. The FEPs perform two primary functions: Routing and flow control. These functions are performed by the NCP software loaded into the machines.

3172 Interconnect Controller

The forté of the 3172 is versatility. It supports a variety of data link level protocols, such as:

- ETHERNET
- 802.3
- 802.5
- 802.4
- Parallel Channel
- FDDI

It can function in a TCP/IP offload offering rather than TCP/IP running upon the host to which it is connected. It can also function as a remote channel-to-channel controller. The versatility and architecture of the 3172 make it a powerful addition to the enterprise hardware line. It is a device that concentrates upon different types of networking architectures. Figure 1.13 depicts a processor and 3172 interconnect controller.

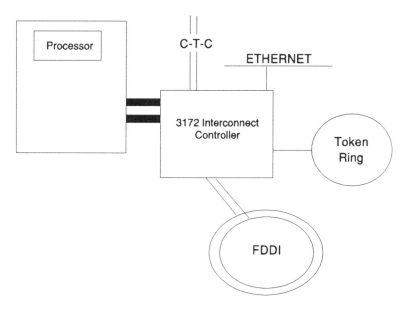

Figure 1.13   Processor and 3172 Interconnect Controller

Storage Devices

IBM offers storage devices such as the following:

- Direct Access Storage Devices (DASD)
- Reel-to-reel tape drives
- Cartridge tape drives
- CD ROM storage devices

These devices have undergone generational changes along with many of the architectural changes. Most of these devices are compatible with multiple architectures. In light of SNA, these devices are not a large component from a conceptual perspective. But, where appropriate, they will be discussed in further detail.

1.6   A Perspective on Software Architecture and Virtual Storage

IBM designed and created numerous software packages through the past 28 years, but the focus here is operating systems. In the beginning (around the 1964 timetable) there was diversity! There still is for the most part, but today IBM's large operating systems can be narrowed to three; these include:

- Multiple Virtual Storage (MVS)
- Virtual Machine (VM)
- Virtual Storage Extended (VSE)

Before examining the parallel between the hardware and software architecture, a brief description of these operating systems is in order.

Multiple Virtual Storage (MVS)

MVS is an operating system. Its name describes its characteristics. MVS means it has built within itself the capability to accommodate multiple users, performing multiple tasks, simultaneously (or at least it would appear that way to a user). The appearance of this phenomenon is because of virtual storage.

The Concept of Virtual Storage

If virtual storage is a new concept for you, do not feel alone. It is not mysterious, nor above your ability to understand. Virtual anything means it appears to exist, but in reality does not. It is a concept, not a tangible thing. It appears to exist and to *be* real because of functionality.

Storage on the other hand is real, meaning it is tangible. Large IBM systems such as those being discussed in this book consist of basically two types of storage; they are:

- Memory—also known as core memory, or better known as real memory. (I have often wondered what unreal memory might be.) Anyway, this type memory is volatile and generally considered internal.

- Storage—a media type such as disks, reel-to-reel tape, cartridge tape drives, or some other method that is generally held as not being volatile and considered external to the processor.

Other names for storage exist, but for the most part those names depict an *implementation* of memory. For example, expanded storage is made up of the same components that core or real memory consist of, but the functionality of expanded storage is different than core or real memory. Memory is memory; what differs is how it is implemented and the addressing scheme.

Consider these comments in light of virtual storage. Data and programs are tangible. If true, then where do these reside in light of virtual storage since we know virtual storage does not exist? Data and programs are located internally in (real) storage or external storage, such as a disk drive, or they are in-between (even if for only a millisecond). Technically, data or programs are in virtual storage when part is in internal storage, part in external storage, and/or en route to one or the other. By definition all of data, or a program, could be in internal or external storage and be classified as residing in virtual storage.

This is possible because moving data or programs from one place to another entails paging (moving a part of data and/or a program) or swapping (moving all data and/or a program to external storage). Virtual storage is achieved via processor speed, internal storage, and external storage. These three ingredients combined create the essence making virtual storage possible.

Because of virtual storage, MVS provides users with the illusion they are performing their "own" functions alone. Additionally, MVS means a multiple number of tasks are supported concurrently. MVS components include an Input/Output (I/O) Supervisor, like a "traffic cop" of I/O for example. MVS also includes a number of utilities that make operations such as copying data sets (files) possible, a number of system utilities that make updating software fixes possible, and of course actual software code that interacts with hardware and microcode (IBM's name for firmware) possible.

MVS is a large operating system, and it was designed to operate with some of the largest hardware IBM ever architected. Because of this its size is not a negative issue. MVS is complex, and therein lies its beauty. Complexity, designed appropriately in operating systems, can translate into power, and MVS is powerful. Figure 1.14 depicts the MVS operating system with multiple users attached using the system.

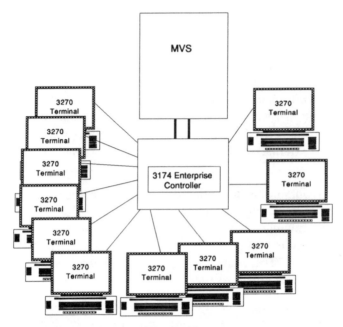

Figure 1.14   MVS Operating System and Terminal Users

MVS is also generally considered a production type operating system; this in contrast to being a software development oriented type operating system. MVS has been the work horse supporting large software subsystems for years and with each release becomes more powerful and refined.

MVS System Product (SP) began with the S/370 architecture. Subsequent releases of MVS, such as MVS/XA, included support to exploit 370/XA architecture. Likewise, MVS/ESA exploited the ESA/370 architecture, and the latest release exploits S/390 architecture.

Virtual Machine (VM)

The VM operating system began with a different design intent than MVS. Whereas MVS supported multiple users performing multiple tasks simultaneously, VM took that concept one step further. VM was architected to simulate multiple machines, supporting multiple users, performing multiple tasks simultaneously. If you are new to VM, you are probably asking what does this mean, and why?

VM was designed with a slant towards supporting multiple operating systems. Operating systems running under the control of VM are known as Multiple Preferred Guests (MPGs). Each MPG can perform distinct functions. It is VM that provides the ability to isolate each operating system from the other. Conceptually, a general diagram depicting this would appear as figure 1.15.

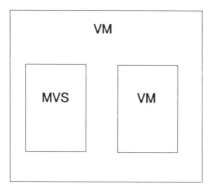

Figure 1.15   VM Operating System and Multiple Preferred Guests

Assume a software development company exists and has the need to provide programmers with multiple operating system support because they are designing, writing, and testing code for different operating systems. How can this need be accomplished?

One way is to purchase as many different hardware systems as needed to support the number of operating systems for development and/or testing purposes. This becomes costly very quick, and one would seek another way to solve this problem. Here is where VM offers its services.

VM has the capability of permitting multiple Preferred Guest (MPG) operating systems to execute simultaneously. This means that MVS can operate under the control of VM. It also means that VM can operate under the control of VM, and likewise with other operating systems that are supported as MPGs. It also means each guest operating system can operate its respective software subsystems simultaneously and independently of any other Multiple Preferred Guest.

This environment is advantageous because any MPG could crash and would not affect others running under VM control. From a software development standpoint this is important. VM, like MVS, has numerous software subsystems that can operate under its control. VM does not require MPGs, that capability is just a feature of VM.

VM like MVS has its base component, the System Product (SP). VM/XA and VM/ESA are also available which correlate to the aforementioned hardware architectures. Other components and IBM licensed products exist and relate to the VM product, however they are not the focus of discussion here.

Virtual Storage Extended (VSE)

VSE, also known as Virtual Storage Extended/Advanced Function (VSE/AF), is the smallest of the three operating systems. But, its size should not be deceptive because VSE is robust. VSE got its name from DOS/VSE, an earlier product in the 1970s. It has the reputation for being flexible, reliable, and user friendly compared to MVS and VM. However, VSE has its own nuances.

IBM has enhanced VSE to operate with its ESA architected machines, thus putting VSE on the same footing as MVS and VM. This author is aware of a reliable study indicating some 30,000 VSE installations worldwide. This installation base is significant, in anybody's terms.

VSE has traditionally been viewed as a production based operating system, smaller than MVS. It has been considered ideal for situations requiring robustness in moderately sized environments.

IBM is continuing to show support for the VSE operating system. According to the February 9, 1993 Customer Announcement Letters from IBM, they announced a cooperative software offering with OpenConnect Systems, Inc. In summary, this announcement underscored IBM's commitment to connectivity issues with the VSE operating system and TCP/IP networks. According to the announcement, OpenConnect Systems will provide the connectivity components to make VSE operable with other vendor equipment just as MVS and VM operating systems are capable of doing so.

1.7 Conclusion

SNA is a large networking environment. IBM created it and continues to refine it. The terms and concepts used in SNA were also created by IBM. In short, SNA is a "world" unto itself.

It is based upon hardware and software architectures. IBM has offered five (5) hardware architectures since 1964. The dominant hardware architectures now are ESA/370 and S/390.

These architectures are implemented in various equipment such as processors, communication controllers, enterprise controllers, interconnect controllers, terminals, printers, and other devices. These architectures are also implemented in software IBM offers such as operating subsystems, telecommunication access methods, and other subsystems supporting the SNA environment.

IBM designed operating systems to work with different hardware architectures. Three major operating systems have emerged over the past decade; they are:

- MVS
- VM
- VSE

These operating systems are unique. Each offers strengths based on their original design intent. They were not originally conceived to be alike or even offer many of the same services. As a result, they operate best in environments that are close to their strengths.

Chapter 2

Software Components
in SNA

As explained in chapter one, SNA consists of hardware and software components. Chapter one focused upon hardware architecture and the major operating systems. This chapter focuses on major software subsystems used in SNA networks. Two categories of software subsystems are identified: First, communication subsystems such as the Virtual Telecommunication Access Method (VTAM) and the Network Control Program (NCP). Second, user oriented subsystems providing interactive, batch, and other processing facilities.

2.1 VTAM: The Heart of SNA

Virtual Telecommunications Access Method (VTAM) is the heart and soul of SNA. Even with the "new" SNA, VTAM is still a major part. VTAM is a software subsystem that operates under MVS, VM, and VSE operating system environments. Its basic purpose in hierarchical SNA is a mediator between software and services inside a processor and requesting users outside the processor. Beyond this it also serves as the controlling point of an SNA network. It performs other functions, and some of those include:

- Controls resources such as software within a processor.

- Provides services for resources outside a processor. For example, it helps terminals connect logically to an application.

- Performs SNA control functions, such as exchanging SNA commands with other nodes in an SNA network.

- Maintains tables of parameters for nodes outside the processor, such as printer characteristics, terminal types, and other resources.

VTAM performs tasks beyond this list. Here it is important to understand the basic role of VTAM so understanding other topics is easier. Figure 2.1 depicts how VTAM appears conceptually.

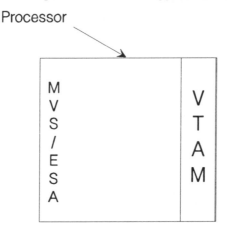

Figure 2.1   Conceptual View of VTAM

As shown in figure 2.1 VTAM is a software subsystem operating under the control of an operating system; in this example, MVS is the operating system.

Chapter 5 discusses VTAM in greater detail. Before examining VTAM functions and how it interacts within an SNA network, it is important to understand some basic concepts and terms first. The following section presents a highlight of three VTAM applications. The purpose of presenting these applications is to orient you to the useable resources within an SNA network. Other application subsystems exist, but they are not the focus of this book.

2.2   VTAM Applications

Users use applications that run within a processor and under the control of VTAM. These applications are also called subsystems and

VTAM applications, with the latter used to refer to smaller programs running under the control of VTAM. For example, consider figure 2.2.

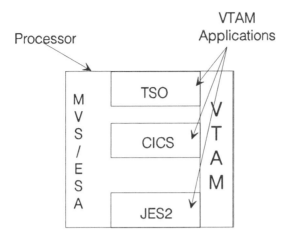

Figure 2.2   How VTAM Applications Appear

In figure 2.2 three application subsystems are shown. Each of them is briefly explained.

JES2

Job Entry Subsystem 2 (JES2) is a spooling subsystem. It is also referred to as the primary subsystem. It is like a waiting room. Before exploring the waiting room, we should discuss what can be in the waiting room. Things to be printed under MVS are called Jobs. So are things to be stored to disks, stored on cartridge tape, sent to another processor, and the like. All these things are referred to as jobs. Jobs have a tendency to increase in proportion to the number of users and size of environment.

As with most waiting rooms, things waiting (be they human or not) somehow tend to get a number attached to them so order can be maintained. So it is with JES. Each job in JES has a number associated with it. By this number a job can be expedited, deleted, or terminated from the processor console.

TSO

IBM's Time Sharing Option (TSO) is an interactive facility made up of three distinct operating environments; they include:

- Line Mode
- Interactive System Product Facility (ISPF)
- Information Center Facility (ICF)

TSO has its origins in Line Mode. In this mode TSO commands can be entered and functions performed. A large number of TSO commands exist, permitting support for services such as:

- Listing a user's data sets
- Printing a data set
- Allocating a data set
- And commands customized to invoke user written applications

TSO's ISPF is a menu driven facility. The menu offers a variety of functions that can be performed. For example, data sets can be created, browsed, edited, and even deleted. Other functions can also be performed via this menu.

An editor is supported under ISPF. Here it is possible for a user to create a program, report, or whatever, just as one might do on a PC. Really, the only difference is the power behind the machine and software package. ISPF also provides general maintenance facilities. It supports the ability to precisely define the amount of storage allotted to data sets, the type record format supported, and where they are to be stored.

Through ISPF a knowledgeable user can browse disk drives and determine what data/programs are stored on them. A tutorial is also included in ISPF, to aid learning the environment.

TSO's Information Center Facility provides a way to access numerous services. It too is menu driven and some capabilities it offers are:

- News service
- Names directory
- Utility programs
- Problem reporting
- HELP information

Other services are available, but the point here is to get a snapshot of what ICF provides.

CICS

Customer Information Control Service (CICS) is an interface between custom application programs, database managers (such as one under IBM's DB2 program offering), and VTAM. In another way it can be viewed as a general manager working with transaction programs.

Consider one possible example of CICS implementation. Suppose you need some money (you are not alone). You go to a local Automatic Teller Machine (ATM), insert your card, and go through procedures to receive cash. Your bank may not even be in the same city as the ATM machine you use. So, how does the machine know it's ok to give you the money you requested? One possible way is for that ATM machine to be logically connected to your bank and have a program locally communicating with CICS (located at your bank's computer). In actuality, two programs are communicating with one another; one locally, in the vicinity of the ATM, and the other operating with CICS at your bank. This is but one example of how CICS can operate, others exist.

IBM has a broad offering of subsystems supporting a variety of needs. These subsystems, like the aforementioned, are large. In fact, they can be thought of as operating systems in their own right. But, for clarity sake, MVS, VM, or VSE are the operating systems and other subsystems technically run under their control. An analogy can best explain these software packages that operate within a processor. MVS is similar to the CEO of a corporation, VTAM is like the president, and other application subsystems are like vice presidents. The vice presidents probably have managers operating underneath them. Granted the analogy is somewhat crude, it is similar!

Another communications component needs examination. It is the Network Control Program (NCP). The following section explains fundamental aspects of an NCP.

2.3 Network Control Program (NCP)

The NCP is a controlling software program and resides in a communication controller node. Conceptually, it appears as figure 2.3.

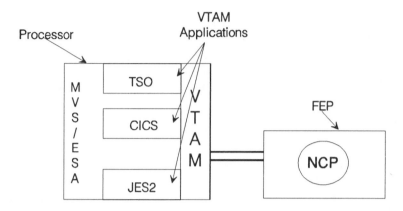

Figure 2.3   NCP Software in an FEP

Its basic purpose includes performing a number of functions. An overview of some of those functions include:

- Controlling communication lines between devices in the network
- Maintaining tables reflecting characteristics of devices throughout the network
- Performing routing
- Performing flow control
- Implementing priority levels on defined routes
- Performing error recovery

Some of the supporting programs NCP supports include:

- Network Packet Switched Interface (NPSI)
- Network Terminal Option (NTO)

These programs operate under the control of the NCP. Each of them provides services. For example, NPSI causes X.25 connections to appear to the NCP as one or more switched or nonswitched SDLC links. In essence, it serves as the interface with an X.25 network. The latter, NTO, supports certain non-SNA based terminals.

Basically, the NCP in conjunction with the communication controller node perform a considerable amount of network operations. The NCPs know of devices attached to the communications controller, thus a device physically connected to one FEP can be routed to another FEP en route to a processor. Consider figure 2.4

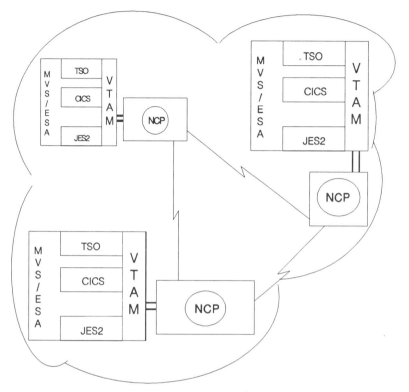

Figure 2.4

This example (figure 2.4) shows multiple FEPs each with an NCP. Also, multiple hosts are shown in different locations. The collection of this hardware and software, including assumed locally based hardware not shown, makes up the SNA cloud.

2.4 Conclusion

Tangible components in SNA include software. VTAM and NCP are the major communications software components of SNA. In addition, application subsystems provide users services such as interactive development facilities, database support, spooling support, and others not mentioned in this chapter.

The following chapters in this book focus more upon explaining the abstract concepts and terms of SNA. This chapter and chapter one provide background information necessary to explore the meaning of the concepts and terms that make up SNA.

Chapter 3

SNA Concepts

Systems Network Architecture (SNA) is a networking protocol (world) unto itself. It was created by IBM. Everything that is a part of SNA was created by IBM: Hardware, software, terminology, concepts, protocols, method of operation, and so forth. Discussions about SNA may include terms that reflect hardware or software mentioned previously and/or reflect some SNA concept. Conversations about SNA can consist purely of terms and concepts that reflect SNA in its most abstract nature. When this is the case, understanding these terms and concepts becomes critical. This chapter begins explaining some of those terms and concepts.

In order to tackle SNA and bring it down to size it is presented topically. After sufficient topics are presented they are synthesized.

3.1 The Concept of a Node

A node in SNA is generically defined as an end point in a link. Better still it can be defined as a device of some kind. Either way a node refers to a tangible thing. Because of the evolution of SNA, two categories of nodes are clearly discernible. These categories refer primarily to the function(s) of a node. First, is hierarchical oriented nodes. Second, are peer oriented nodes.

Hierarchical Oriented Nodes

Traditional SNA was hierarchical in respect to function. Practically any function performed went through the hierarchy. Simply put, the access method (VTAM) had the lion share of control within the network. Without it there was no network.

The first type node in this hierarchical based network is a *host node*. It is a processor. The processor has an access method in it. It controls certain nodes in the network. Figure 3.1 depicts a host node.

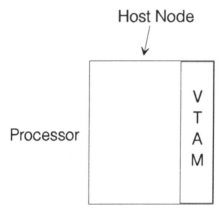

Figure 3.1   A Host Node

Figure 3.1 is a generic reference to any processor with an access method in it. Typically, this access method has come to be known as VTAM. In years past other access methods existed, but VTAM is by far the dominant access method among IBM's "mainframes."

The second type node is a *communications controller node*. It is as its name implies, a communications processor. It has an NCP in it. Figure 3.2 shows a host node and a communications controller node.

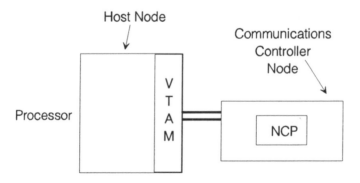

Figure 3.2   Host and Communications Controller Nodes

Whereas figure 3.2 shows only one communications controller node, it is possible that multiple nodes of this type could be connected to a processor.

The third type node is a *peripheral node*. Generally speaking, peripheral nodes are the source and/or destination of data. For example, a 3174 establishment controller and a 3270 type terminal attached would be considered a peripheral node. Figure 3.3 shows a peripheral node, communications controller node, and host node as they appear in a typical installation.

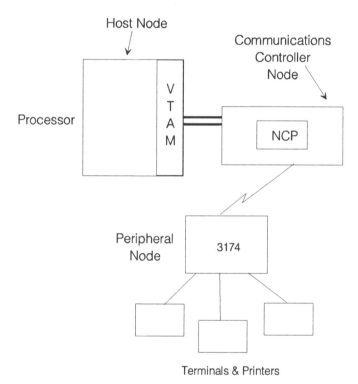

Figure 3.3   Peripheral Node

Understanding these three nodes makes it possible to understand network devices and label them according to SNA terminology.

These examples reflect traditional SNA in a hierarchical arrangement. This type network still exists today, but SNA is evolving into a peer oriented type network. But for the foreseeable future, both hierarchical and peer type SNA nodes will coexist.

Peer Oriented Nodes

The concept of peer oriented nodes removes the notion that a centralized (hierarchical) arrangement is necessary. These type nodes permit communication without the intervention of a host node.

The notion of peer nodes is derived from Advanced Peer-to-Peer Networking (APPN). APPN has its own architectural definitions. And, it is from these definitions that peer nodes get their identity. IBM has identified three types of peer nodes.

First, is the *network node*. A network node (also referred to as NN) provides certain network related services for other nodes attached to it. For example, a network node maintains a directory of all applicable network resources. It can also participate in a hierarchical type SNA network as a peripheral node. The determining factor for what device can function as a network node is that device's architecture.

To provide a list of devices that can function as networking nodes could be misleading. For example, a 3174 establishment controller can function as a network node. However, it would be incorrect to conclude that a 3174 can only function as a network node. It can, and frequently does, function as a peripheral node in hierarchical SNA.

Another characteristic of a network node is it can perform dynamic route calculation for routing purposes and also dynamic resource searches. So, what does this mean? Really, all this means is that NNs have the ability to search on-the-fly and determine the best route for a session to be established and where a particular resource is located.

Of the three types of peer oriented nodes, the NN is the smartest of the three; meaning it has the ability to perform more functions. It is architecturally different.

The second type peer node is an *APPN End Node*. This type node has limited directory and routing services. It does have the capability to choose an adjacent network node to provide these functions. Operationally, when a request is made at an APPN End Node the request is passed onto an appropriate network node. APPN End Nodes can have more than one NN to which they have connections. A characteristic of the APPN End Node is that it has the capability to communicate with an NN via a certain type logical connection that performs management functions. Herein lies the main difference between it and a *LEN End Node*.

The third type peer node is a *Low Entry Networking (LEN) node*. This type node can be attached to a network node and hence indirectly to an APPN network. This type node can also be attached to another LEN node. If so, it can communicate with this other LEN node on a peer basis. Unlike the APPN End Node, it cannot establish the type logical connection with a network node required for that LEN node to register its resources with an NN.

3.2   The Concept of Subareas

A confusing aspect of subareas occurs when one understands no *areas* exist. This seems odd. In most anything when there is a sub-something, it implies a "something" else above it in some type of order. Not true within the realms of traditional SNA or the peer oriented SNA. The roots behind this is that IBM created SNA.

To eliminate as much confusion as possible, a subarea will be defined according to IBM's *Dictionary of Computing*, #SC20-1699-8:

> "A portion of the SNA network consisting of a subarea node, attached peripheral nodes, and associated resources. Within a subarea node, all network addressable units (NAUs), links, and adjacent link stations in attached peripheral or subarea nodes that are addressable within the subarea share a common subarea address and have distinct element addresses."

This baseline part of the definition can shed light upon aspects being focused upon here.

In a hierarchical network the following subareas can be defined by *nodes*, previously explained.

- A processor (host node), alone, constitutes a subarea.
- A communications controller node and attached peripheral nodes also constitute a subarea.

An example of these two subareas is shown in figure 3.4.

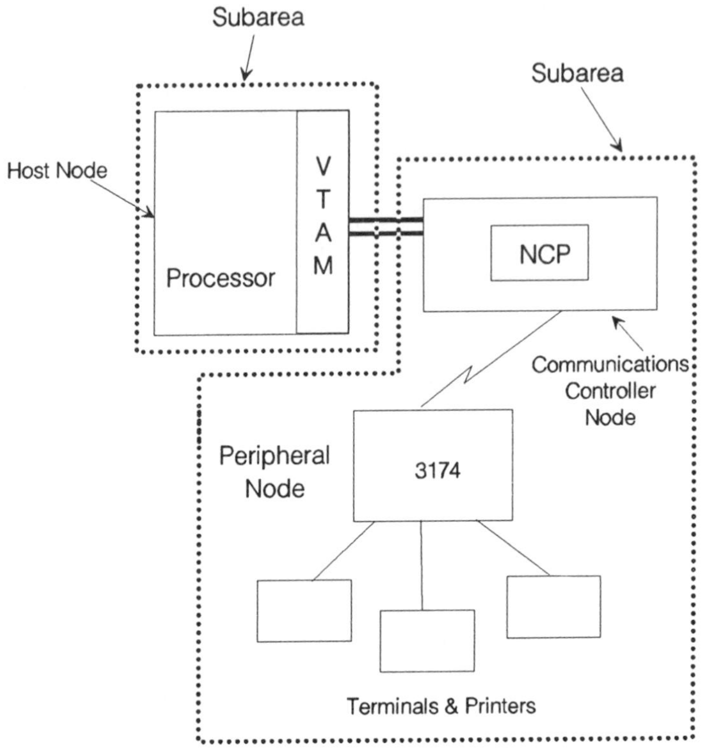

Figure 3.4   Two Distinct Subareas

Figure 3.4 shows a host node as a subarea. It also shows a communication controller node and a peripheral node (including attached devices such as terminals and printers). The point of figure 3.4 is that two distinct subareas exist.

Figure 3.4 also represents a subarea network. The definition of a subarea network is one that consists of (at least) the aforementioned subareas. Thus, an additional statement can be made about figure 3.4. Collectively, it can be referred to as a subarea network.

An aspect related to subareas will be presented later, but additional information must be covered first to lay proper foundation for understanding this concept called a *Domain*.

3.3 The Concept of Network Accessible Units (NAUs)

In SNA the concept of network accessible unit (NAU) exists. NAUs are addressable entities within the network. Different NAUs consist of the following:

System Services Control Point (SSCP)

The SSCP is a part of VTAM. Specifically, it is a module of VTAM software. It performs management functions like bringing up and down a Domain. (Domains will be discussed in greater detail later. Suffice it that they are parts of subareas.) The SSCP assists in establishing and terminating sessions (logical connections) between NAUs. It also performs other management functions such as reacting to network devices that report problems. In traditional hierarchical networks the SSCP is responsible for establishing logical connections between users and application subsystems. Consider figure 3.5 depicting the location of the SSCP.

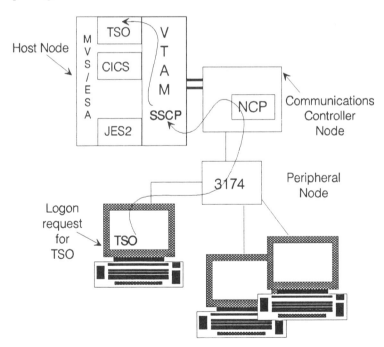

Figure 3.5   The SSCP and VTAM

Control Point (CP)

This is the focal point that manages resources in APPN nodes. It provides optional services to other valid nodes within the network. In some ways a CP is similar to an SSCP. The CP manages the overall resources within a node. Some examples of what it does include: creating path control and data link components. Additionally, the CP communicates with other CPs in network nodes to obtain what network services are available. It also assists Independent Logical Units (these will be explained shortly) in session initiation and termination.

Physical Unit (PU)

Physical Units are not *physical units*! Technically, a PU is a portion of a tangible device. The PU is implemented in the device via software or circuitry in some cases. A PU exists in processors, communication controllers, establishment controllers, cluster controllers, and enterprise controllers to name a few. It performs control functions for the device in which it is located. Each device in an SNA network is associated with a particular PU. PUs play a role in activation and deactivation (to be discussed later), error recovery, resynchronization, testing, and collecting statistics about the operation of the device it is located within. Consider figure 3.6 showing a PU in various devices.

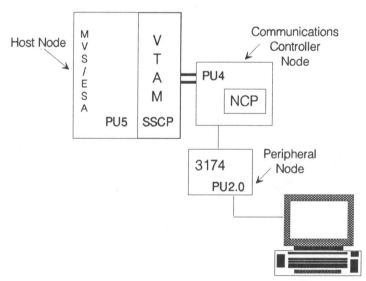

Figure 3.6   Where PUs Appear

Logical Unit (LU)

This is an addressable end point. An LU is also considered an entry point into an SNA network. Application subsystems have LUs defined so they may interact with another program, terminal, or other device. These devices (printers, terminals, etc.) are known to the SNA network as LUs. Examples of types of LUs will be forthcoming.

3.4 Types of Physical Units

As described previously, PUs are defined and implemented in software or circuitry and provide capabilities to perform controlling functions in physical devices. PUs manage links, link stations, virtual and explicit routes in PU type 5 and 4 nodes, and the PU is the recipient of requests from SSCPs and CPs. The following lists PU types and nodes they are implemented within:

- PU Type 5—Host nodes (Processors)
- PU Type 4—Communication Controller nodes
- PU Type 2.0—3174 Establishment Controller nodes
- PU Type 2.1—ES/9000 Processors, APPN nodes, and others

PUs can be explained according to their characteristics. Consider the following:

- PU 5—Is capable of supporting all types Logical Units. PU type 5 nodes are considered host nodes.
- PU 4—A PU type 4 node is primarily responsible for routing and flow control. It is a communications controller node.
- PU 2—This type PU supports dependent logical units. This means an SSCP is required to aid in session establishment.
- PU 2.1—This type PU supports independent logical units. It means an SSCP is not required for session establishment.

3.5 Types of Logical Units

SNA has defined different types of logical units (LUs) which perform different functions. In the most general use of the word, a Logical Unit (LU) is an addressable end point in an SNA network.

Two categories of LUs include:

- Dependent LUs (DLUs)
- Independent LUs (ILUs)

Dependent Logical Units (DLUs) require an SSCP to aid in session establishment. This type session is where the application subsystem functions as the Primary Logical Unit (PLU) and the terminal (LU) is considered the Secondary Logical Unit (SLU).

Independent Logical Units (ILUs) do not require an SSCP for session establishment. This type LU is peer oriented and supported by PU5, PU4, and PU2.1 nodes.

Consider the following LUs and their basic characteristics:

- LU0—This uses non-SNA protocols. Custom applications can be written using LU0 protocol.
- LU1—This supports SNA Character String and Document Content Architecture. Some applications use LU type 1 for printing.
- LU2—This is used by applications and workstations in an interactive environment using the 3270 data stream protocols.
- LU3—This is a 3270 data stream used by 3270 type printers.
- LU4—The SNA Character String uses this type LU. Peripheral nodes communicating with each other and certain distributed processing environments use this LU.
- LU6.1—This type LU is used between application subsystems communicating with another in a distributed processing environment.
- LU6.2—This LU supports user defined data streams or the SNA General Data Stream. It supports sessions between two or more applications in a distributed environment. This type LU supports multiple, concurrent sessions. This LU is defined and used with peer program communication.
- LU7—This type LU supports a 5250 data stream used in the AS/400 environment.

3.6 The Concept of a Domain

A *domain* in SNA is an area of control. Domains differ between hierarchical (subarea) networks from APPN networks. In a subarea network (one that has a PU type 5 node) a domain is that portion of the network managed by the SSCP in the access method. See figure 3.7.

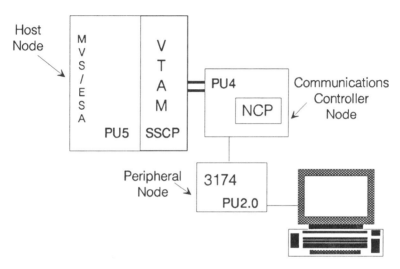

Figure 3.7   Single Domain Network

In figure 3.7 a host node, communication controller node, and peripheral node are shown. Notice the type PU reflected by each device. This example is called a single domain network.

In an APPN network a domain is that part of the network *served* by the control point in a node. For example, in an NN the CP may serve an APPN END node and LEN END node.

Figure 3.8 is an example of a multiple domain network.

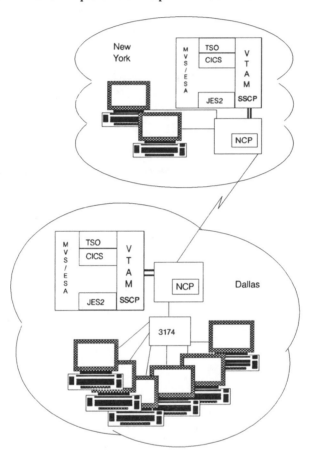

Figure 3.8   Multiple Domain Network

In a multidomain network at least two processors exist, each with an SSCP. In a subarea network where multidomains exist the concept of cross domain resource sharing is possible (and will be examined later).

3.7   Types of Sessions

In SNA a session is a logical connection between two end points. Different types of sessions have been defined and perform different functions. Some sessions are used in establishment and maintenance of devices within a network. Other sessions are logical connections used to interact with applications. Still other sessions are used by programs to communicate with one another.

The following is a list of session types defined in SNA and their basic function.

SSCP-to-SSCP—This is used by PU 5 nodes to communicate with one another for purposes of establishing cross domain sessions.

An SSCP-to-SSCP session is required before a user in one domain can access resources in another domain. Conceptually, an SSCP-to-SSCP session appears like figure 3.9 depicts.

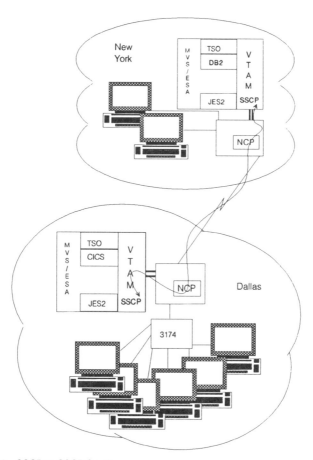

Figure 3.9   SSCP-to-SSCP Session

CP-to-CP—This is used between two control points exchanging information necessary prior to LU-LU sessions. This type session is characteristic of APPN networking nodes; in essence the CP is the controlling point in APPN nodes.

In an APPN network, NN's CPs communicate with one another across a CP-to-CP session to exchange information and parameters necessary for operation. Consider figure 3.10.

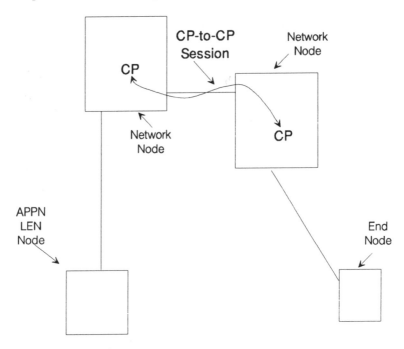

Figure 3.10 CP-to-CP Session

SSCP-to-PU—This session is used initially to send the SNA Activate PU (ACTPU) from the SSCP. This command causes a particular PU to become active.

In a subarea network, before a device can be used it must be activated. To activate a device requires the appropriate SNA command be sent from the SSCP to the PU across an SSCP-to-PU session. Figure 3.11 provides an example of this.

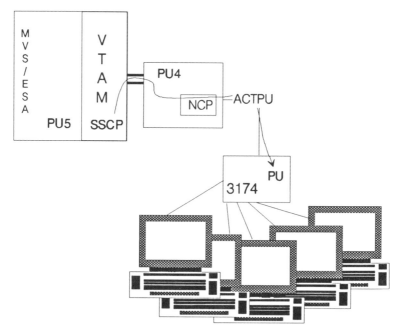

Figure 3.11   SSCP-to-PU Session

Activating a device (PU) is accomplished when a VARY command is entered and received by VTAM. Once the VARY ONLINE command is issued against the desired PU, the SSCP sends the ACTIVATE PU (ACTPU) command to the target PU.

SSCP-to-LU—This session is used to send the SNA command activate logical units (ACTLU) to the LUs in a given device. This command causes particular LUs to become active.

In a subarea network, before logical units can be used they must be activated. To activate them requires the appropriate SNA command be sent from the SSCP to target LUs. This may be performed by sending the command across an SSCP-to-LU session. Figure 3.12 provides an example of this.

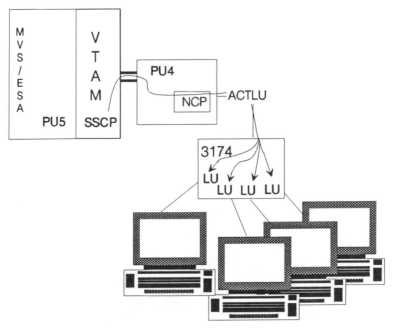

Figure 3.12 SSCP-to-LU Session

LU-to-LU—This is a user to user session. An example of this type
   session is a user loging on to an application; once logged in, an
   LU-to-LU session exists.

Prior to a LU-LU session, a request must be sent to the SSCP in a
subarea network to request session establishment with a particular
application subsystem. This type request is generally entered by
selecting a choice from a menu displayed on the terminal. Consider
figure 3.13.

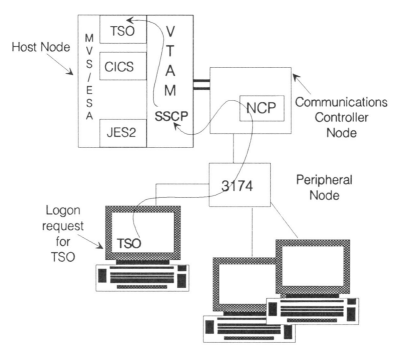

Figure 3.13   Example Logon Command

Figure 3.13 shows a user entering a command to log on to TSO. The request is passed to the SSCP in VTAM, then on to TSO. The SSCP aids in the establishment of the session between the terminal user and TSO.

3.8   Types of Links

SNA supports different types of data links. Termed link in SNA nomenclature, the meaning behind the word is, "to connect two nodes." The following is a list of types of links supported in traditional SNA and the new IBM networking blueprint.

Parallel Channel—This is a type of processor. The connection is made via two copper stranded cables, called BUS and TAG. The parallel channel is IBM's new name for what was called channel. The name changed with the announcement of Enterprise System Connection (ESCON). The parallel channel is also known as the S/370 data channel. The parallel channel can accommodate high data rate transfers. It transmits data in parallel from source to destination. Typically, these type channels can operate up to 200 feet maximum, when daisy-chained.

ESCON—The acronym for Enterprise System Connection, this is IBM's fiber optic based subsystem comprising the media, physical, and data link portion of the network. ESCON is used with ESA/390 (S/390) architecture, can transmit up to 17 million bytes per second, span over 14 miles (over 26 miles with additional control units and over 37 miles with chained ESCON directors to another channel), consists of 2 conductors per interface, and supports up to 1,024 device addresses per path. An ESCON environment consists of an ESCON I/O interface, ESCON Manager, ESCON directors, fiber optic cable, ESCON channel, and an ESCON director console.

Token Ring—Physically implemented via a Media Access Unit (MAU), the actual ring is inside the MAU. Token Ring technology is available in 4 or 16 megabit offerings. Token ring technology is connection oriented at the data link level. Token ring technology is ideal in large environments where it can be used in flow control and routing. See figure 3.14.

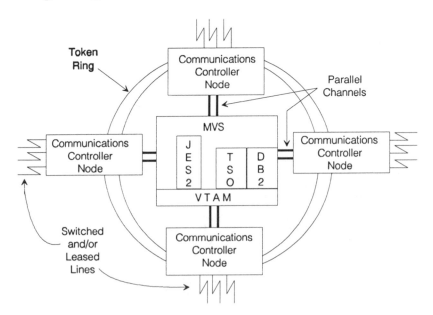

Figure 3.14   Flow Control with Data Links

It is also an ideal LAN technology because it is relatively inexpensive and very reliable. It is fault tolerant, meaning nodes can be inserted and removed from the MAU at will without disrupting data transfer. It is considered a self-healing technology.

SDLC—The acronym for Synchronous Data Link Control, it is a prevalent method for connecting nodes via telecommunication lines. SDLC is a bit oriented protocol providing robust data transfer. It is mature and prevalent in the marketplace.

FDDI—The acronym for Fiber Distributed Data Interface, this is a high speed data link level protocol; typical data rates are 100 megabytes per second. It is an industry standard and is accepted throughout the world. Some specific IBM products now support this protocol.

ETHERNET—Some specific IBM devices now support ETHERNET as a link connection. ETHERNET, as described earlier in the book, is a broadcast technology, capable of using thick or thinnet coaxial cable or copper twisted pair cabling. Technically, ETHERNET is a data link level protocol implemented in firmware (microcode) on network interface boards.

X.25—A packet switching technology. IBM has supported this for a number of years. X.25 is prevalent in many parts of the world. Certain software packages are required to support this technology in SNA.

3.9 Conclusion

SNA consists of many abstract concepts. Depending upon the implementation, even specific terms such as nodes take on different meanings in different implementations. Understanding some concepts requires knowing how other concepts and terms relate. For example, subareas and domains are closely related, but they are different. Network addressable units are fundamental to most concepts in SNA and APPN; therefore, it is important to know what these NAUs do and their characteristics. Links are important to understand because different types of links are supported in SNA. Sessions are still another important concept to grasp in order to delineate functions of each. These concepts, and others in this book, are critical to understanding the meaning behind the abstract concepts that are pertinent to SNA.

Chapter 4

SNA From Past to Present

Systems Network Architecture (SNA) past to present is presented in this chapter. The purpose of this chapter is to orient the reader to where SNA is in respect to its evolution over time. Not all SNA announcements and products have been included, but those thought to have had significant impact on SNA.

4.1 SNA in the 1970s

SNA's first version was primitive when compared to today's standards. It was a strictly hierarchical implementation. Consider figure 4.1.

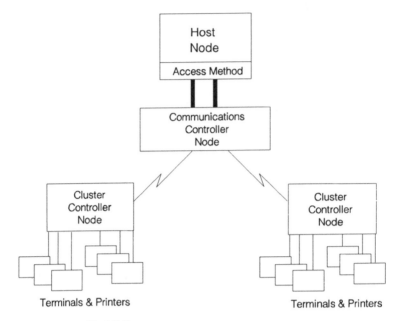

Figure 4.1   Hierarchical SNA

SNA, as announced in early 1975, seemed to be the first real public commitment and was the next logical step in its evolution. This version of SNA implemented a star type arrangement of communications controller nodes. This provided the capability for a remote communications controller node. But with the introduction of a star based communication controller node environment came an interesting irony. In a scenario where a remote communications controller node was located, only non-SNA devices were supported in the remote location. See figure 4.2

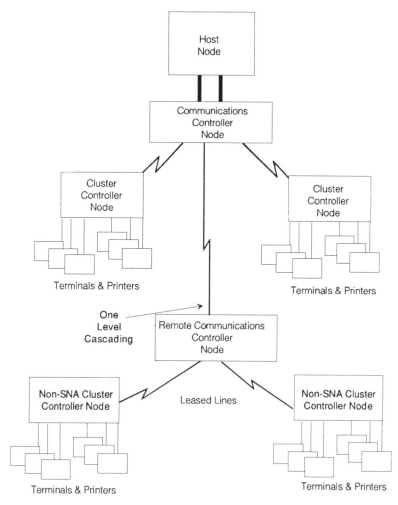

Figure 4.2   Non SNA Support in Remote Locations

SNA's next iteration in late 1975 offered the following:

- Remote communication controller nodes could support SNA as well as non-SNA devices.
- Cluster controllers (those which terminals and printers attached) could now be channel attached to the host via bus and tag cables.
- Cluster controllers and terminals could be attached to communication controllers by way of leased or switched telephone lines.
- More than one communication controller nodes could be attached to the same host.
- A remote communication controller could be attached to a locally attached communication controller node via a leased line. This has been referred to as cascading (specifically, one level). Figure 4.2 depicts this scenario.

In 1977 IBM announced another release of SNA. It followed previous releases adding functionality in numerous areas. For example, support for SNA connection to X.25 packet switched networks was announced. Another break-through was the ability of an application in one host to communicate with an application in another host. This was probably the first "peer" implementation, and this release touted multiple host support via connection through communication controller nodes with leased lines or data channels as shown in figure 4.3.

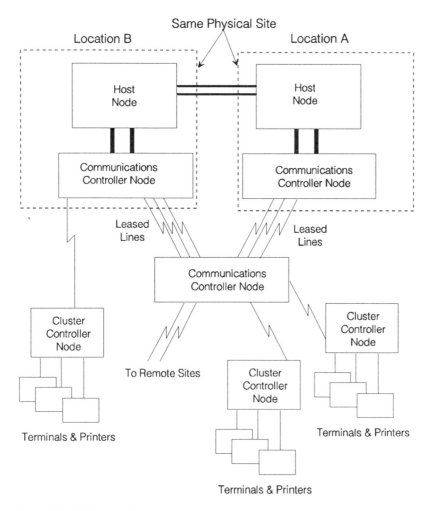

Figure 4.3   SNA Peer Implementation

A break with SNA of the past occurred with the 1978 announcement. A big feature was that communication controllers cascaded beyond one level. This was significant. See figure 4.4.

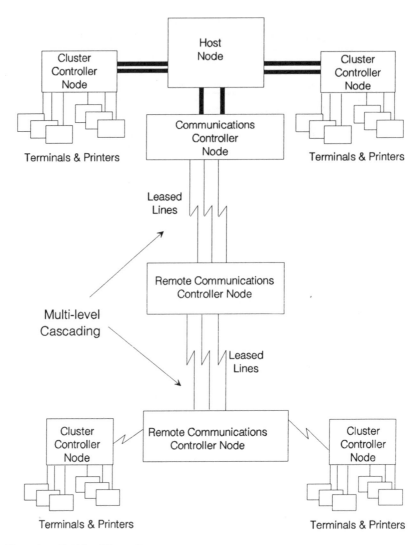

Figure 4.4 Multi-level Cascading

In 1978 the Communications Network Management (CNM) facility was added to the SNA network program offerings. These offerings focused on providing a centralized control within an SNA network for management facilities. The CNM announcement included a base function provided through the Network Communications Control Facility (NCCF). This was a valued addition because it supported execution of VTAM commands. Another application contributed additional abilities through which a network operator could identify, isolate, and monitor problems throughout the SNA network. This application, called Network Problem Determination Application (NPDA), made a step towards managing large networks spanning multiple physical locations. Examine figure 4.5 to understand conceptually NCCF and NPDA.

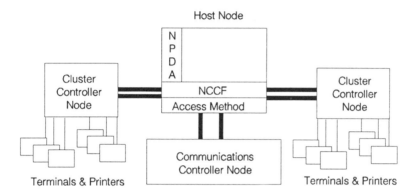

Figure 4.5   NCCF and NPDA Conceptually

The 1979 announcement brought additional contributions to SNA; they included, parallel links and multiple routes that were supported between communication controller nodes and hosts. This enhancement was a great contribution because of implications it had on routing and throughput. Consider figure 4.6 as it depicts this.

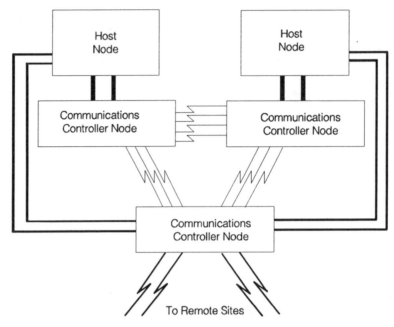

Figure 4.6   Parallel Links and Multiple Routes

In addition to the example in figure 4.6, other contributions were made to SNA in the 1979 time period. For example, the capability to perform session cryptography (session level security), network terminal option (NTO), a program supporting certain non-SNA devices, and parallel sessions. Parallel sessions are two or more simultaneously active logical connections (sessions) between two logical units (LUs) achieved via different network addresses. Around this same time period (1979 to 1980) X.21 support was announced for SNA (some consider it to be a 1980 product).

The 1970s witnessed the birth and immediate growth of SNA in supporting products and acceptance in the marketplace. History has proven the 1970s period was merely the beginning for SNA compared to the whirlwind of development in the following decade.

4.2 SNA in the 1980s

Due to the amount of enhancements and contributions in the 1980s, the following list of products, features, and functions are simply correlated to the basic time frame when they were introduced. This is not an attempt to list all announcements of products and services, just enough to show the reader where some major product offerings were introduced on a time scale.

1980	X.21 protocol support, System Services Control Point (SSCP) takeover in cross domain environments (two subareas with VTAM), transmission priorities, parallel links, and multirouting capability became available.
1981	IBM announced its first Personal Computer PC.
1981	First architectural definition of LU6.1 was announced.
1981	Announcements relating to sessions between logical units were made.
1981	The Network Packet Switched Interface (NPSI) supporting SNA to SNA connectivity and SNA to non-SNA connectivity via X.25 support was introduced.
1981-1982	Advanced Program-to-Program Communication (APPC) became available.
1982	Document Interchange Architecture (DIA) was announced.
1982	Document Content Architecture (DCA) was announced.
1983	SNA Network Interconnection (SNI) was announced.
1983	Type 2.1 node architecture, Document Interchange Architecture (DIA), Peer Communications, and Non-SNA Interconnection (SNI) were announced.
1984	SNA Distribution Services (SNADS) was introduced.
1984	3270 emulation support for PCs was announced.
1984	VM operating system and SNA became functional together.
1984-1985	A new addressing scheme was announced for SNA supporting up to 8 million addresses in one SNA network. This was referred to as Extended network addressing.
1985	Network Design and Analysis was announced.

1985	Token Ring and SDLC support was announced for PU2.1 architecture.
1985	PC support for APPC/LU6.2 was announced.
1986	Token Ring LAN support in an SNA environment was introduced.
1986	NetView was announced as the network management framework.
1986	Advanced Peer-to-Peer Networking (APPN) was announced for the S/36.
1987	NetView PC was announced. This permitted NetView to manage non-SNA and SNA devices.
1987	Systems Application Architecture (SAA) was announced.
1987	The Personal System2 PS/2 was announced.
1987	IBM's Operating System2 OS/2 was announced.
1988	The AS/400 was announced.
1988	NCP support for VM and VSE operating system support was announced.
1988	NCP support for T1 lines was announced.
1989	The 3172 LAN-to-Channel controller was announced.
1989	Support for casual connections was added to VTAM Version 3 R.3.
1989	Casual connection support through subarea nodes was supported.

Systems Application Architecture Announcement

In March 1987 IBM introduced its System Application Architecture (SAA). It is broad, encompassing products, architectures, and general development direction. It created a flurry of questions and general uncertainty in the marketplace because SNA users did not (and still do not) know how to respond to such sweeping announcements. SAA is a software based architecture designed to operate with certain operating systems; they include:

- OS/2
- OS/400
- MVS
- VM

The basic components of SAA include:

- Common User Interface (CUA)
- Common Programming Interface (CPI)
- Common Communications Support (CCS)

In essence SAA is a collection of protocols, user, programming, and communication interfaces defining how an information system is built. The basic components of SAA previously listed are three interfaces. With these interfaces, SAA can be achieved. This provides a common approach to a user interface, programming, and communications.

Basically, CUA defines standards focusing on ergonomics. It provides consistency and some level of intuition built into the standard. This means a user interacting with OS/400 will have fundamentally the same look and feel interface as a user interacting with a MVS operating system. This common interface is the goal behind CUA.

CUA is achieved by using common terminology across different platforms and interaction techniques. CUA is based on windows, title bars, action menus, and scroll bars. The interface was designed with clerical users, service representatives, management, and development personnel in mind.

CPI is the programming interface. It supports software development languages such as C, COBOL, or FORTRAN; and the most common being the C language. This interface specification is focused with the Information System (IS) professional in mind. This interface can be used by programmers to develop applications in any of the aforementioned languages. The CPI goal is akin to CUA; that is, to provide a common interface between the user (programmer in this case) and the system.

CCS is the communications interface; it defines formats and protocols thus allowing standardization across any SAA supported platforms. CCS includes data link level protocols that are defined in SNA, ISO, CCITT, and the IEEE. This provides broad options for the developer. The CCS part of SAA is critical because it is the foundation for communication between any SAA based systems.

4.3 SNA in the 1990s

Since 1990 IBM has unleased a number of products and services on the marketplace that have changed SNA. It has been evolving, but since 1990 the changes are quite significant. Some of the announcements include:

1990	S/390 architecture
1990	Enterprise System Connection Architecture (ESCON)
1990	Sysplex Timer
1990	MVS/ESA Version 4 R.1 & R.2
1990	Micro Channel 370
1990	VTAM Version 3 R.4 for MVS/ESA, VM/ESA, and VM/SP
1990	OSI interoperability support
1990	SystemView
1991	The Information Warehouse Framework
1991	APPN support added to 3174
1992	6611 multiprotocol router
1992	APPN support added to VTAM
1992	VTAM Version 4 R.1
1992	Command Tree/2 for VTAM Version 4. R.1
1993	18 new ES/9000 processors
1993	MVS/ESA Version 4 R.3 OpenEdition Services including a subset of IEEE POSIX
1993	DB2 Family of products including Database 2 for the AIX/6000

Other products and services have been announced and brought to market since 1990, but they are too many to list here. The purpose here is to focus on some major product offerings.

4.4 Traditional SNA Layers

Until the IBM announcement in 1992, the structure of SNA could be examined from a layered perspective. Because of different variations of SNA in the marketplace, it is beneficial to understand the layered

SNA model. Figure 4.7 presents SNA layers, and the explanation following makes the layered concept less abstract.

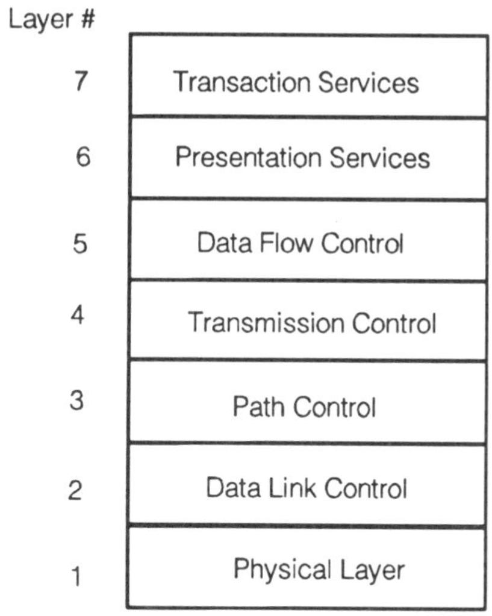

Layer #

7	Transaction Services
6	Presentation Services
5	Data Flow Control
4	Transmission Control
3	Path Control
2	Data Link Control
1	Physical Layer

Figure 4.7

SNA layer names, functions, and related components are explained below.

Physical Control

This is the lowest layer defined in SNA. It consists of interface cards or ports where media attach physically making connections to other entities within the SNA network. This SNA layer generates the electrical or photonic pulses necessary for transmission.

Data Link Control

The data link control layer is responsible for transmitting data between nodes. This layer is responsible for determining data format and passing it to the physical layer when en route to the target host. Conversely the data link control layer assimilates data back into the format on the target host and passes it upward to the path control layer. Data flow control occurs at layer 2, along with establishing, maintaining, and terminating logical links.

Path Control

This layer is responsible for routing data between source and destination nodes. Software plays a major role here; specifically, the Virtual Telecommunications Access Method (VTAM) and the Network Control Program (NCP). This layer is responsible for regulating data traffic in the network; for example, selecting transmission groups, virtual routes, and explicit routes.

Transmission Control

This layer is responsible for pacing data between source and destination nodes within the network. Software determines much of this function. Specifically, VTAM and NCP work here. In addition, data security is provided at this layer if desired.

Data Flow Control

This layer synchronizes data exchange and arranges data into units defined according to the rules of SNA. Software determines these functions also.

Presentation Services

This layer is responsible for determining data format. Syntax of data is determined here. This layer is where resource management occurs.

Transaction Services

This layer provides application services for application subsystems to operate. It also provides services supporting distributed databases and data interchange between nodes.

SNA architecture is based upon hardware and software as previously mentioned. Examples of hardware components to achieve this include:

- Processors
- Distributed Processors
- Communication Controller Nodes
- Enterprise Controllers
- Interconnect Controllers
- Workstations
- Printers

Software components used to achieve SNA implementation include:

- Operating Systems
- VTAM
- NCP
- Application Subsystems

4.5 IBM's Networking Blueprint

IBM announced its networking blueprint in 1992. It is a clear break from IBM's historical networking approach because it embraces more than traditional ways of SNA networking. For example, it states support for the following upper layer protocols:

- SNA/APPN
- TCP/IP
- OSI
- NetBIOS, IPX, and others.

Figure 4.8 depicts IBM's networking blueprint.

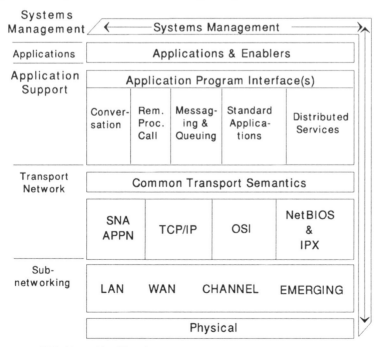

Figure 4.8   IBM's Networking Blueprint

If nothing but the upper layer protocol support changed, this indicates a radical break from IBM's past, but this is only the beginning. The networking blueprint transforms how IBM approaches networking.

If the new IBM blueprint is contrasted with the traditional layered model, interesting observations can be made. First, the networking blueprint supports SNA. Second, it embraces TCP/IP, OSI, and other upper layer protocols. Ironically, it does not propose to solve existing dilemmas between disparate protocols, it merely states support for them. In all fairness, IBM does have the technical wherewithal to solve the technical problems, thus resolving disparate protocol problems. But, in essence, IBM is saying, "Here's what we'll do. We'll offer, and support, popular industry protocols, providing a cafeteria style approach to networking." IBM appears to have proposed a networking blueprint capable of accommodating popular networking technologies, at all network layers, and marketed them in a new fashion.

In a very real sense IBM has bought an insurance policy by embracing this blueprint. Since it includes a variety of networking protocols and nonproprietary network services/support, IBM is no longer bound to their traditional proprietary method of networking. IBM can now compete with popular industry networking protocols.

A synopsis of the IBM networking blueprint reveals:

Systems Management—Spans the blueprint from top to bottom, thus supporting different protocols and multivendor environments while providing a cohesive method of performing total network management. Some management protocols include: Simple Network Management Protocol (SNMP), X/Open Management Protocol (XMP), and SystemView to name a few.

Application Services—Also known as standard applications, this part of the blueprint includes multivendor application service support. The thrust here is provision for application transparency whether local or remote with respect to the user, thus providing true distributed application support.

Application Program Interface (APIs)—These provide necessary hooks bridging applications to the Application Support Layer.

Application Support Layer—Applications operating higher in the blueprint require support. Basic application support includes three defined areas according to the blueprint. They include:

- Message Queue—This manages queues of messages.
- Conversational support—This deals with handling streams of related interactions.
- Remote Procedure Call—Its function is passing parameters to subroutines.

For clarification sake, TCP/IP's TELNET, FTP, and SMTP reside at the application layer. They are a part of the TCP/IP networking protocol. Additionally, distributed services are located at this layer.

Common Transport Semantics—Herein lie functions linking applications to transport layer protocols. Actually, common transport semantics and transport network services fall into the same category, but they are delineated, isolating transport layer mechanisms to maximize the needs of application requirements. Because of this, multiprotocol routing is easily supported.

Subnetwork Layer—This encompasses data link protocols and physical layer standards. Figure 4.8 shows multiple data link level protocols are supported, providing flexibility to choose existing data links while preserving room for growth and accommodating emerging technologies at this layer. Physical layer support is broad. Support includes many variations of hard media as well as soft media such as satellite and microwave.

4.6 Conclusion

SNA has gone from birth to adulthood in nineteen years. It is in a constant state of flux. SNA has its own formats and protocols, but these are implemented via hardware and software.

Latest announcements about SNA seem to indicate that it is opening up and evolving into another network protocol supported in the overall networking blueprint. At this point in time it appears that SNA, TCP/IP, and OSI will comprise the lion share of networking in the coming years.

Chapter 5

VTAM Basics

VTAM is a major part of SNA. In traditional, hierarchical SNA VTAM was basically the center of network operations. This is changing as SNA evolves and products providing expanded services become available. However, 3270 terminal users accessing VTAM applications still use VTAM in the traditional sense. This chapter does not attempt to explain all there is to know about VTAM. It explains what VTAM is, some of its components, and what these components do. Knowing this will make comprehending chapter six easier.

5.1 A Primer

VTAM is a software subsystem as explained in chapter two. It is a partitioned data set (PDS). Conceptually, it appears like figure 5.1.

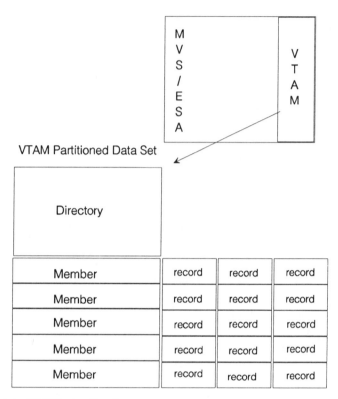

Figure 5.1   VTAM System Data Set

The partitioned data set consists of three parts. The first is the directory. It is a listing of members. Members are similar to files. Data for each member is stored in records. A simple analogy of a partitioned data set is simply a directory and files.

Different type data sets exist in an MVS operating environment. The one important to this discussion is a SYSTEM data set. A *system* data set provides system services for overall functions within a network. This type data set uses a SYS1 for a prefix. For example, the VTAM PDS is typically referred to as SYS1.VTAMLST. It has members providing parameters for applications, nodes in the network, and other supporting functions required for system operation.

Assume the following scenario for our example of VTAM. VTAM has been installed on an ES/9000 processor, MVS is the operating system, and the following subsystems are installed: TSO, CICS, and JES2. Figure 5.2 depicts this.

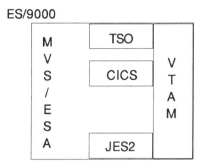

Figure 5.2   VTAM Applications

Assume we want to add a 3174 and some 3270 type terminals. How is this done? Good question!

Assume the correct 3174 and terminals have been purchased. Both the 3174 and terminals have been physically attached to the processor, and the 3174 has been defined to the Input/Output (I/O) subsystem. What remains is defining the 3174 and terminals to VTAM. This is where we will begin exploring VTAM. The physical scenario appears like figure 5.3.

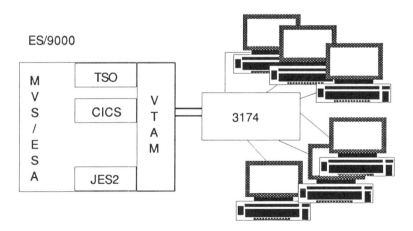

Figure 5.3   Physical View of a Subarea to be Defined

Figure 5.3 shows the physical implementation of this scenario, and it appears like this in a real environment. In addition to being physically attached, logical definitions must be made for the 3174 and terminals to be functional. This logical definition is the focus here. So, what must be defined to VTAM for the 3174 and the terminals in our example to operate?

5.2 Device Definition

Regardless of the device, be it a 3174, 3274, 3745, 3172, etc., it must be defined to VTAM appropriately. Yes, this is the "I gotcha." The *appropriate* manner, that is.

VTAM programming is complex. Many variations are possible to define devices. Generally speaking, the larger the network, the more complex are VTAM definitions. This is why our example is one 3174 and a few terminals.

To know how to define a device to VTAM requires understanding:

- VTAM programming to a certain degree
- The device to be defined
- The device's function

This sounds straightforward, and in many cases it is once some basics are understood. But, unless one is familiar with these three areas, defining it can be difficult.

We will assume the 3174 supports a few 3270 type terminals needing access to applications running in the processor. Since this is the case, we can define it as a PU2.0. Understanding how a device can be GENed in respect to PU is important. Many devices can be GENed differently. For example, some devices can be GENed as PU2.0 or PU2.1. The term GEN is abbreviated for generation. It refers to a VTAM generation or other generations where a device (or program) is defined.

Understanding SNA concepts and terms is critical when performing a GEN for software and hardware. Knowing what a PU2.0 can and cannot do is critical. And, in most cases the device or application dictates how the GEN is to be performed.

Section 5.1 explained VTAM as a partitioned data set consisting of members. The VTAM PDS is typically referred to as the SYS1.VTAMLST or VTAM PARMLIB.

Network devices require a member (including definitions) in VTAM. Consequently, the larger the network, the larger the SYS1.VTAMLST PDS.

5.3 Defining a Local SNA Major Node

To some extent, VTAM determines the way a device or application is defined. VTAM programming must be used for defining resources. Its syntax must be followed. The focus here is upon requirements for a 3174 with 3270 type terminals attached. A sample GEN defining a 3174 and terminals to VTAM follows. Examine it and notice the three distinct areas or categories.

```
**********************************************************************
*                                                                  *
*                                                                  *
*          Local SNA Major Node Definition Example                 *
*                                                                  *
*                                                                  *
*                                                                  *
**********************************************************************

OUR3174    VBUILD    TYPE=LOCAL


OUR3174PU1   PU      CUADDR=145,          Control Unit Address
                     DLOGMOD=DEFBIND,     Name of Def. LOGMODE
                     ISTATUS=ACTIVE,      Auto ACTIVE
                     MAXBFRU=24,          Buffer size
                     MODETAB=DETBIND,     Name of custom LOGMODE
                     PACING=0,            Pacing is performed
                     PUTYPE=2,            2 is Required
                     SSCPFM=USSSCS,       Unformatted Sys. Serv.
                     USSTAB=DETTAB        Name of USSTABLE
```

OUR317402	LU	LOCADDR=02,	Defining a 3278 m-2
OUR317403	LU	LOCADDR=03,	Defining a 3278 m-3
OUR317404	LU	LOCADDR=04,	Defining a 3278 m-4
OUR317405	LU	LOCADDR=05,	Defining a 3278 m-5
OUR317406	LU	LOCADDR=06,	Defining a 3279 m-2
OUR317407	LU	LOCADDR=07,	Defining a 3279 m-2

This is an example. It is close to a real scenario, but a real site will differ. Notice the three distinct portions of this member. This is due to the nature of VTAM programming. These portions can be called categories; and they include:

- VBUILD statement
- PU statement
- LU statement(s)

This example reflects some definitions required by VTAM for a 3174. An explanation of each category and its components follows.

The VBUILD Statement

The VBUILD statement is the first line in the 3174 in this example. The statement itself has three parts and appears like:

	DEFINITION	
NAME	**STATEMENT**	**OPERAND**
OUR3174	VBUILD	TYPE=Local

The NAME is a symbolic name given to the device and is site dependent. Here it is referred to as OUR3174. The NAME is optional but recommended so the node can be identified by name when VTAM issues messages to it.

The DEFINITION STATEMENT is a VTAM requirement. It will always be VBUILD.

The OPERAND=LOCAL is required to identify the node to VTAM as a local SNA major node. This is important because of how SNA operates and how VTAM "sees" this device.

PU Statement

The PU statement is also required. It follows the VBUILD statement. An example of it appears like:

NAME	DEFINITION STATEMENT	OPERAND
OUR3174PU1	PU	CUADDR=
		DLOGMODE=
		ISTATUS=
		MAXBFRU=
		MODETAB=
		PACING=
		PUTYPE=
		SSCPFM=
		USSTAB=

The previous PU statement does not include all possible operands that can be used. These listed are frequently used. The following explains what they mean.

First, the CUADDR operand reflects the parallel channel and subchannel address. This number is written in Hexadecimal notation. The first number is the parallel channel number. The following two numbers are the subchannel address. To understand this concept consider this analogy.

I live in a house on a street. We will refer to the street as XYZ. Specifically, I live in a house on XYZ street. My house has an address; it is 25. So, if I were to tell you where I lived, I would say, "I live at 25 XYZ street." The analogy is thus: The street name is analogous to the parallel channel number, and my house address is analogous to the subchannel address.

In a real installation, a parallel channel may have multiple devices attached to it. Hence, it would appear as a street with multiple houses. Consider figure 5.4 depicting a parallel channel with multiple devices each having different subchannel addresses. The cabling connecting these devices are called bus and tag cables.

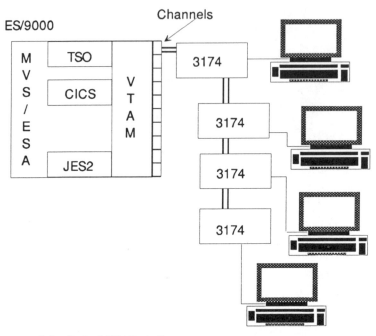

Figure 5.4   Daisy-Chained 3174 Controllers

This example shows a parallel channel connecting multiple 3174s via bus and tag cables. These 3174s are connected in daisy-chained fashion.

The second operand is DLOGMODE. DLOGMODE is the name of another member in the SYS1.VTAMLST. It is a table providing session parameters describing how a session must be conducted. In other words it defines session protocols used by LUs. If this operand is not defined, and the name of another logon mode table is not specified, VTAM will use the first entry in the table defined by the MODETAB operand or it will use the IBM supplied default known as ISTINCLM.

The DLOGMODE operand is one of many that utilizes a sift-down effect in VTAM. This means if an operand is coded at a PU level, then all LUs associated with it will use it. The sift-down effect can be overridden, and this will be discussed later when LU operands are explained. The point is if the DLOGMODE operand is coded against the PU statement, then all associated LUs will use it as a default (unless they have a LOGMODE table coded against them individually).

The ISTATUS operand determines whether or not a device will be activated automatically by VTAM. In many cases the ISTATUS= ACTIVE is coded. This causes the PU to activate after the channel is activated. If ISTATUS=INACTIVE is coded, this requires a user to manually vary the device activity.

The MAXBFRU operand specifies the number of buffers VTAM utilizes to receive data from the PU. Hence, a correlation exists between the two. For more information about this operand refer to IBM's VTAM Network Implementation Guide for the current version and release of VTAM. Contingencies exist for this operand, and if not coded correctly a 3174 will not function properly.

The MODETAB operand is an operand whereby a site can define their own LOGMODE table and assign a name to it. When this is done sites usually have specific parameters required for operation. For example, MODETAB=EDLOGMODE would be valid. This operand's parameter named EDLOGMODE points to a member in the SYS1.VTAMLST where entries can be customized as necessary. This example is frequently used because sites differ, and this method of VTAM coding permits customization as needed.

PACING is an operand VTAM uses to determine the rate of data flow from the Secondary Logical Unit (SLU), which is a terminal user in this instance, to the Primary Logical Unit (PLU), which is typically an application subsystem. When the SLU and PLU are in the same domain, this parameter is ignored. If the SLU is in one domain and the PLU is in another domain, VTAM uses this parameter (a numeric value) to throttle data flow. In a sense it is a tuning parameter.

The PUTYPE operand identifies the PU type. In our example we have used PU Type 2.0. This type PU is typical for 3174s. Remember, PU2.0 only supports dependent logical units (DLUs).

SSCPFM is the operand specifying what type data an LU can use with its communication with the SSCP. If USSSCS is coded, this means the LU supports character coded messages with the SSCP.

USSSCS identifies the Unformatted System Services table that VTAM uses to process character coded data from the LU. An USSTAB operand is only valid for dependent logical units.

Other operands may be coded against the PU statement, and they are typically site dependent. The best source for knowing which operand should be coded against a particular device can be ascertained by a combination of that device's installation/customization manuals and IBM's VTAM publications.

LU Statement

LU statements are required. One must be defined corresponding to each LU. It specifies the type LU used and sometimes parameters against an individual operand. An example of some basic LU definitions would appear like:

NAME	DEFINITION STATEMENT	OPERAND
OUR317401	LU	LOCADDR=01
OUR317402	LU	LOCADDR-02
OUR317403	LU	LOCADDR-03
OUR317404	LU	LOCADDR-04
OUR317405	LU	LOCADDR-05
OUR317406	LU	LOCADDR-06
OUR317407	LU	LOCADDR-07

Here LUs are defined sequentially. This is the norm. The LOCADDR operand specifies the LU's address on the device where it is located.

Other parameters can be coded against a specific LU operand; however, they are too many to list here. Their purpose permits an LU to act a certain way or provide a certain function whereas other LUs assume the sift-down effect from the PU. If LUs do not have additional operands coded against them, they will assume the PU operand and parameters by default.

5.4 Defining a LOGMODE Table

A LOGMODE table consists of entries. One entry corresponds to a specific type LU. Each entry defines session parameters for that specific type LU. For example, if a LOGMODE table has an entry for a 3278 M-2 terminal, that entry will specify not only the LU type but other session parameters for all 3278 M-2 terminals. This is important because when a request is made from a terminal user to access an application subsystem, this is where parameters come from to form the

BIND image between the terminal user (LU) and the application; notably referred to as a PLU-SLU session in a device supporting dependent logical units. Consider the following example of a LOGMODE table.

```
**************************************************************
*           THIS IS THE LOGMODE TABLE FOR OUR3174           *
**************************************************************
*         LOGMODE TABLE ENTRY FOR 3278-M2 EMULATION         *
**************************************************************
DETMODE    MODETAB

DETMOD2    MODEENT   LOGMODE=DETM2,
                     FMPROF=X'03',
                     TSPROF=X'03',
                     PRIPROT=X'B1',
                     SECPROT=X'90',
                     COMPROT=X'3080',
                     RUSIZES=X'F8F8',
                     PSERVIC=X'028000000000000000000200'
**************************************************************
*         LOGMODE TABLE ENTRY FOR 3278-M3 EMULATION         *
**************************************************************
DETMOD3    MODEENT   LOGMODE=DETM3,
                     FMPROF=X'03',
                     TSPROF=X'03',
                     PRIPROT=X'B1',
                     SECPROT=X'90',
                     COMPROT=X'3080',
                     RUSIZES=X'F8F8',
                     PSERVIC=X'028000000000185020507F00'
**************************************************************
*         LOGMODE TABLE ENTRY FOR 3278-M4 EMULATION         *
**************************************************************
DETMOD4    MODEENT   LOGMODE=DETM4,
                     FMPROF=X'03',
                     TSPROF=X'03',
                     PRIPROT=X'B1',
                     SECPROT=X'90',
                     COMPROT=X'3080',
                     RUSIZES=X'F8F8',
                     PSERVIC=X'02800000000018502B507F00'
**************************************************************
*         LOGMODE TABLE ENTRY FOR 3278-M5 EMULATION         *
**************************************************************
DETMOD5    MODEENT   LOGMODE=DETM5,
                     FMPROF=X'03',
                     TSPROF=X'03',
                     PRIPROT=X'B1',
                     SECPROT=X'90',
                     COMPROT=X'3080',
                     RUSIZES=X'F8F8',
                     PSERVIC=X'02800000000018501B847F00'
**************************************************************
*                   DETMODE    MODEEND                      *
**************************************************************
```

Understanding LOGMODE table entries is not as difficult as it appears. The following is a brief explanation of the parameters defined in our example. For clarity sake, the first entry will be used, that is, a 3278 M-2.

The MODETAB=DETBIND operand (used in our example previously) points to a member named DETBIND in the SYS1.VTAMLST. This member contains special session parameters for specific LUs. In the previous example of a LOGMODE table four entries have been used (one for a 3278 terminal model 2, 3, 4, and 5).

The FMPROF operand defines data flow protocols used between the LU-LU session.

The TSPROF operand defines session rules for the traffic flow between Primary Logical Units (PLUs) and Secondary Logical Units (SLUs).

The PRIPROT defines SNA protocol details for functions such as responses, etc.

The SECPROT provides information used for the bind process. Specifically, it provides data relating to the Secondary Logical Unit (SLU).

The COMPROT defines common protocols used during primary and secondary half sessions between LUs. A primary half session sends the session activation request. A secondary half session receives (or is the target of) the session activation request from the primary half session.

The RUSIZE defines the amount of data inbound and outbound to the Primary Logical Unit (PLU).

The PSERVIC operand specifies the LU type, data stream support, and screen size for terminals.

5.5 The USSTAB

The Unformatted System Services table (USSTAB) is a (SYS1.VTAMLST member), considered a facility used by the SSCP. It translates logon or logoff requests into field formatted requests required by the formatted system services. By this a site can customize a banner screen and have a *logo* visible on 3270 type terminals, or any valid terminal. It is this member in the SYS1.VTAMLST from which the banner screen is generated.

In order to establish a session with an application a terminal user sends a logon request to VTAM. In SNA field formatted requests are used. This means a logon or logoff is formatted to what the system expects. However, other logons, such as entering an application name like TSO, are not field formatted.

Because of this an unformatted system services table must be defined to interpret the request and match it to the appropriate parameters so they can be passed, invoking the desired application. This TSO request specifies the name of a desired application. The USSTABLE supplies the required logon mode name and applicable user data.

In summary, if a site wants users to see a menu on their terminals and enter a command like TSO and that application be invoked, then a USSTABLE will have to be coded.

The focus here is understanding the major parts of the USSTABLE (which will be explained after the example is shown). The example is accurate in basic structure, but alterations would need to be made in a real environment. Consider:

```
********************** TOP OF DATA ***************************
*                                                            *
*************    USSTAB TITLE 'DETUSS TABLE'   ****************

DETUSS      USSTAB

LOGON       USSCMD   CMD=LOGON,FORMAT=PL1
            USSPARM  PARM=APPLID
            USSPARM  PARM=LOGMODE
            USSPARM  PARM=DATA


VM          USSCMD   CMD=VM,REP=LOGON,FORMAT=PL1
            USSPARM  PARM=APPLID,DEFAULT=VM
            USSPARM  PARM=LOGMODE
            USSPARM  PARM=DATA


TSO         USSCMD   CMD=TSO,REP=LOGON,FORMAT=PL1
            USSPARM  PARM=APPLID,DEFAULT=A01TSO
            USSPARM  PARM=LOGMODE
            USSPARM  PARM=DATA
```

```
CICS            USSCMD  CMD=CICS,REP=LOGON,FORMAT=PL1
                USSPARM PARM=APPLID,DEFAULT=DETTCCICS
                USSPARM PARM=LOGMODE
                USSPARM PARM=DATA


JES2            USSCMD  CMD=JES2,REP=LOGON,FORMAT=PL1
                USSPARM PARM=APPLID,DEFAULT=JES2
                USSPARM PARM=LOGMODE
                USSPARM PARM=DATA



USSMSG MSG=0,TEXT='USSMSG0:   @@LUNAME LOGON/LOGOFF IN PROGRESS'
USSMSG MSG=1,TEXT='USSMSG1:   @@LUNAME INVALID COMMAND SYNTAX'
USSMSG MSG=2,TEXT='USSMSG2:   @@LUNAME % COMMAND UNRECOGNIZED'
USSMSG MSG=3,TEXT='USSMSG3:   @@LUNAME % PARAMETER UNRECOGNIZED'
USSMSG MSG=4,TEXT='USSMSG4:   @@LUNAME % PARAMETER INVALID'
USSMSG MSG=5,TEXT='USSMSG5:   @@LUNAME UNSUPPORTED FUNCTION'
USSMSG MSG=6,TEXT='USSMSG6:   @@LUNAME SEQUENCE ERROR'
USSMSG MSG=7,TEXT='USSMSG7:   @@LUNAME SESSION NOT BOUND'
USSMSG MSG=8,TEXT='USSMSG8:   @@LUNAME INSUFFICIENT STORAGE'
USSMSG MSG=9,TEXT='USSMSG9:   @@LUNAME MAGNETIC CARD DATA ERROR'
USSMSG MSG=10,BUFFER=MSG10
USSMSG MSG=11,TEXT='USSMSG11:  @@LUNAME SESSION ENDED'
USSMSG MSG=12,TEXT='USSMSG12:  @@LUNAME REQ PARAMETER OMITTED'
USSMSG MSG=13,TEXT='USSMSG13:  @@LUNAME IBMECHO %'
USSMSG MSG=14,TEXT='USSMSG14:  @@LUNAME USS MESSAGE % NOT
DEFINED'



MSGBUFF
MSG10      DC    (MSG10E-MSG10-2)

           DC    C'                              ',X'15'
           DC    C'                              '
           DC    C'        USING THE CORRECT     ',X'15'
           DC    C'                              '
           DC    C'        VTAM SYNTAX YOU       ',X'15'
           DC    C'                              '
           DC    C'        CAN PUT THE BANNER    ',X'15'
           DC    C'                              '
```

```
DC    C'        SCREEN OF YOUR CHOICE    ',X'15'
DC    C'                                 '
DC    C'              HERE !             ',X'15'
DC    C'                                 '
DC    C'                                 ',X'15'
DC    C' ----------------------------- '
DC    C' ----------------------------- ',X'15'
DC    C' YOU CAN CREATE YOUR OWN         '
DC    C'                                 ',X'15'
DC    C'              MENU               ',X'15'
DC    C'                                 '
DC    C'         SO USERS LOGON          ',X'15'
DC    C'                                 '
DC    C'     BY APPLICATION NAME         ',X'15'
DC    C'                                 '
DC    C'              SUCH AS            ',X'15'
DC    C'----------------------------- '
DC    C'              VM                 ',X'15'
DC    C'                                 '
DC    C'              TSO                ',X'15'
DC    C'                                 '
DC    C'              CICS               ',X'15'
DC    C'                                 '
DC    C'              JES2               ',X'15'
DC    C'                                 '
DC    C'-----------------------------'
DC    C'-----------------------------',X'15'
DC    C'                                 '
DC    C'                                 ',X'15'

END      USSEND
*********************** BOTTOM OF DATA *********************
```

Notice three distinct sections exist; they include:

- The logon command and associated parameters. Examples above include LOGON, VM, TSO, CICS, and JES2.
- The VTAM messages. These are message 0 through 14.

- The MSG10 buffer. This is the buffer containing the banner displayed on terminals. Included here is the message displayed on terminals. This example includes logon commands such as VM, TSO, CICS, and JES2.

These three sections comprise most (if not all) USSTABLES. The first part of the table contains applications coded as they are defined to VTAM, necessary parameters to be passed to invoke the application. This is the APPLID= parameter. An example of this is: PARM=APPLID,DEFAULT=A01TSO. When a terminal user enters TSO, these parameters get passed to the TSO application definition in the A01 domain.

The second part of the table are the VTAM messages. They are numbered 0 through 14. They each have a particular meaning; some are more obvious than others. The best source to acquire more information about these messages is in the current VTAM Messages & Codes manual from IBM. This manual has an entire chapter explaining the meaning behind each message.

The last part of the table is that part customized by sites. It is used to display a banner screen and menu of valid application programs users can access by merely entering TSO for example. The example used here is not coded as would be required if this were to be operational. The best reference for finding information on how to customize the USSTABLE is found in IBM's VTAM Resource Definition Reference for the latest version and release of VTAM.

5.6 A Brief on Application Definitions

Application subsystems running in the processor must be defined to VTAM as well. Their definition is similar to other VTAM definitions in that they have basic categories that must be defined. For example, CICS is an application subsystem and its definition to VTAM consists of the following:

- NAME (logical name associated with the application subsystem)
- VBUILD statement
- Operand and associated parameters

An example of a CICS application subsystem definition would be like the following:

```
                DEFINITION
NAME            STATEMENT OPERAND    PARAMETERS
OURCICS         VBUILD TYPE=APPL
```

In a GEN it could appear as:

```
OURCICS    VBUILD  TYPE=APPL


OURCICS    APPL         ACBNAME=
                        AUTH=
                        DLOGMODE=
                        EAS=
                        MODETAB=
                        PARSESS=
                        VPACING=
```

The ACBNAME (Application Control Block Name) is the name an LU uses to establish a session with that application program if it is in the same domain as the application. Technically, the ACBNAME is the minor node name for this application. VTAM uses this control block because it contains data VTAM needs in order to know the application's characteristics.

The AUTH operand is used to determine whether or not this application has authority to use certain VTAM functions. Examples of such functions include:

- Communication Network Management interface (CNM)
- PASS option. This is where an application can pass session establishment requests to other applications

DLOGMODE specifies the name of the default of the logon mode table.

EAS (Estimated Number of Active Sessions) is a numeric value used to estimate the number of concurrent active sessions allowed. Simply, an estimate of LU-LU sessions. IBM VTAM manuals are required in addition to knowing site requirements to provide an appropriate number.

MODETAB is the name of the customized logon mode table.

PARSESS is the operand informing VTAM this application can have multiple concurrent sessions with another application program or Independent Logical Units (ILUs) in the same, or different, domain.

The VPACING operand parameter indicates the number of flow requests another logical unit can send to this application per session before waiting to receive a response.

This example is intended to provide the reader with a basic understanding of application definitions. It is not intended to be a tutorial on VTAM application definition. IBM's VTAM Resource Definition Reference should be used, in addition to other VTAM manuals, when applications must be defined to VTAM.

5.7 How Sessions Are Established

This section explains what happens when a terminal user attempts a logon to an application. It assumes all hardware has been installed and configured appropriately. It also assumes all software used in the example is installed and configured properly. Before examining the sequence of events consider figure 5.5 showing the environment.

ES/9000

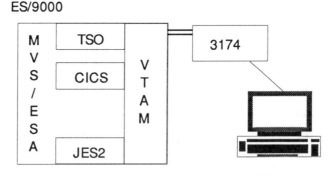

Figure 5.5   Components for Session Establishment

Figure 5.5 shows a processor, MVS as the operating system, TSO, CICS, and JES2, 3174 establishment controller, and a terminal. The explanation will focus upon one terminal performing a logon to TSO.

Figure 5.6 depicts the sequence of events a user performs when attempting to log on to TSO. Examine figure 5.6.

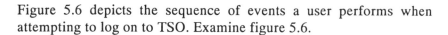
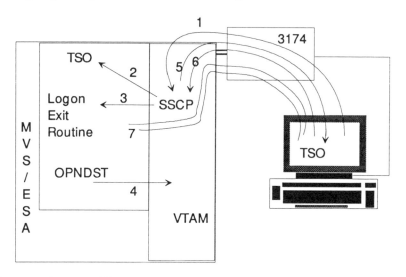

Figure 5.6   Sequence of Events Used to Log On to TSO

First, [1] a user enters TSO then presses the Enter key. When the Enter key is pressed, the logon data is considered an Initiate request. This is passed to the SSCP. The SSCP scans the USSTABLE for TSO. When it finds TSO, the SSCP translates the TSO logon into Initiate Request format.

Second, [2] after the SSCP has received the Initiate Request it contacts TSO via a Control Initiate (CINIT) request via an SSCP-LU session. The SSCP passes data from the original Initiate Request and session parameters in the Control Initiate (CINIT) request. TSO examines any data received and session parameters. In layman's terms the SSCP tells TSO, hey, there is a terminal user wanting to go into session with you.

Third, [3] VTAM schedules execution of TSO's LOGON exit routine. The SSCP uses this exit routine to inform TSO it should establish a session and act as the Primary Logical Unit (PLU). Once this operation is performed, the TSO's LOGON exit routine either accepts or rejects the CINIT.

Fourth, [4] if accepted, the OPNDST macroinstruction is issued by TSO. This macroinstruction is passed back to VTAM.

Fifth, [5] VTAM builds the BIND request for the LU requesting the session and passes it to that LU.

Sixth, [6] assuming the requesting LU agrees with the BIND image, it sends a positive response back to the SSCP.

Seven, [7] upon receipt of a positive acknowledgement from the requesting LU, TSO and the requesting LU enter a session. In this case TSO is the PLU and the terminal user is the SLU.

These steps are what occur unseen to the user. This is how sessions are established in an environment where dependent logical units are used and nonnegotiable BINDs are implemented. Granted this seems to be a lengthy endeavor, but the entire process happens in fractions of a second.

5.8 Conclusion

By now it is obvious there is more to VTAM than meets the eye! The focus in this chapter has been on concepts and how some aspects of SNA work. This chapter has presented basic information about VTAM and related topics. It is not intended to replace IBM's VTAM manuals, but it does orient the reader to VTAM and some related aspects.

Chapter 6

A Perspective on APPN

One of APPN's confusing aspects is that "everything" seems to be a node. The node concept is nebulous. This chapter explains some APPN topics and concepts mentioned previously in the book. Because of the scope of APPN, limited information will be presented, but it is pertinent in light of SNA.

6.1 The Nebulous Nodes

Node types in an APPN environment can be referred to as Type 2.1 nodes. Multiple Type 2.1 nodes exist. We begin with three including:

1) An APPN Network Node

2) An APPN End Node

3) A LEN End Node

Before exploring APPN and other related type nodes, some information should be presented about these three nodes just mentioned. Basic characteristics about these three nodes include:

APPN Network Node

- Provides support services for its end users
- Provides directory services for its end users

A directory (in APPN) includes resource names such as logical units and the Control Point (CP) name of the node where resources are located. The directory is maintained by an APPN node, and that node manages searches within that directory for resources.

- Provides route selection services

Route selection is a Type 2.1 facility that determines the best route for data traffic between two nodes given a particular class of service. A class of service provides information such as transmission priority, route security, and other needs for a particular session.

- Provides Management Services

Management services includes performance, accounting, config-uration, and change management.

- Intermediate Routing

This is a function of an NN that allows it to receive and route data that is neither destined for that node nor originates from it. It performs an intermediary role in a routing scheme.

- Performs Distributed Searches

An APPN NN performs the distributed service function to locate LUs that may be remotely located within the network. It also uses this function to determine the best route for origin to destination based on user supplied criteria.

- Provides Network Node Server Functions

This role of an NN serves APPN End Nodes and/or LEN End Nodes, in addition to its own local LUs. Its primary purpose in this network node server role is to provide directory services and route selection as mentioned previously. Consequently, it is considered an NN server.

APPN End Node

- Registers their local LUs as an NN server

This means a network operator at the NN does not have to predefine LU names for LUs in the APPN End Nodes. The registration function is dynamic.

- Support for multiple NN connections

APPN End Nodes can be attached to multiple NNs. The functionality of the APPN End Node with NNs permits only one Control-Point-to-Control-Point (CP-to-CP) session at a time. However, the benefit of this feature is that it provides backup for a function.

- Provision for Limited Directory Services

An APPN End Node can provide its LUs with limited directory services. It is capable of performing these functions by its Control Point CP communicating with its NN server's CP and exchanging requests for directory services.

- Provision for Limited Route Services

As with limited directory services, so the APPN End Node can exchange information with its NN server's CP concerning limited routing services. It can acquire information pertaining to routing. Hence, it is capable of provided routing services in a limited fashion.

LEN End Node

The LEN End Node implements basic Type 2.1 end node protocols. A fundamental characteristic of a LEN End Node is connections made by it to remote LUs must be predefined by system definition. Another characteristic is that it can attach to other LEN End Nodes via peer protocols. Also, it can attach to a subarea network as a peripheral node.

6.2   The Type 2.1 Node Advantage

One of the strengths that Type 2.1 architecture provides is support for Independent Logical Units (ILUs). Independent Logical Units do not require VTAM to manage their session. LU6.2 is currently the preferred LU used in Type 2.1 nodes, but these nodes do support other LUs as well. Figure 6.1 below shows an LU6.2 session between two Type 2.1 nodes. It also shows a separate scenario where an LU 2 terminal session accesses TSO, and VTAM is required to manage the session.

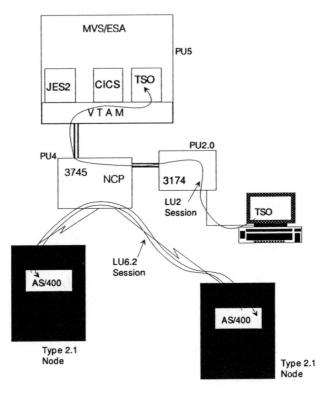

Figure 6.1   An Lu6.2 Session Between Two Type 2.1 Nodes

In figure 6.1 both traditional, hierarchical SNA and an APPN (peer) implementation are shown. The hierarchical SNA concept includes a PU2.0 device and a terminal. In this example, the terminal is accessing TSO via LU2. LU2, by definition, is a dependent LU, so VTAM is required to aid in session establishment and management.

The peer concept (utilizing Type 2.1 architecture) implements LU6.2 for a session. LU6.2 is an independent LU. It does not require the intervention of VTAM to establish a session, nor does it need VTAM for session management.

Type 2.1 nodes can be implemented in different devices. Some of those devices include:

- AS/400
- S/36
- VTAM and NCP together
- VTAM alone

Other devices such as a TCP/IP-to-SNA gateway can be a T2.1 node if it has been architected to act as such. This list is just an example to provide some tangible information to this concept of a node.

6.3 APPN Nodes and VTAM

APPN and Type 2.1 nodes were not originally associated with VTAM. However, over time IBM began to bring them together. For example, with VTAM Version 3 Release 2 and NCP Version 4 Release 3.1, VTAM and an NCP could operate together and "appear" as what is known as a composite LEN node.

This example of VTAM and NCP, including associated hardware, made up what is called a subarea network. VTAM, NCP, and the hardware were the subarea network in the sense of traditional (hierarchical) SNA. With these versions and releases of VTAM and NCP Type 2.1 support was provided for Type 2.1 devices connected to this subarea network. Hence, VTAM and NCP was considered a composite LEN node because of the support it provided.

As time passed and versions and releases changed, VTAM supported Type 2.1 nodes to a subarea network without an NCP. VTAM Version 3 Release 3 provided this support. With this version and release of VTAM a Type 2.1 device could attach directly to a channel via an integrated communication adapter (ICA) and communicate with VTAM applications or other Type 2.1 devices.

Casual Connections

A VTAM node can be defined as a Type 2.1 node. As mentioned previously, VTAM and an NCP acting as a composite LEN node can be defined as a Type 2.1 node. When a VTAM node and a composite END node are connected via logical connection, this is called a casual connection. A casual connection can occur when one or more of the following have been defined:

1) Two composite LEN nodes have been defined to each other as Type 2.1 nodes.

2) A VTAM node and a composite LEN node are defined to each other as Type 2.1 nodes.

3) Two VTAM nodes are defined to each other as Type 2.1 nodes.

Some of the benefits of casual connections include:

- Defining a cross domain resource manager is eliminated.
- Explicit path definitions are not needed.
- Virtual route definitions are no longer required.
- Cross domain resources need not be defined.
- The need for multiple SSCP tables is eliminated.
- Overall, less definition is required.

However, with the advantages of casual connections requiring fewer definitions overall, limitations do exist. The intent of casual connections was not to replace the SNA backbone. It was merely to provide additional functionality on a peer basis.

The bottom line is a casual connection equates to a peripheral node connection. Hence, only one link exists. To deduce further: no virtual route is possible, no explicit route definition is required, and no cross domain session can be established because of the nature of the node support. Consequently, understanding the intent behind casual connections is prudent.

VTAM V.4 R.1 and APPN

The point to understand with VTAM Version 4 Release 1 and its support of APPN is that VTAM can now perform two roles. For example, in versions and releases prior to V.4 R.1, VTAM was considered a subarea node. In essence it operated in a hierarchical manner. It had to have routes, resources, and other aspects of the network manually defined.

Now, with APPN support it can still operate as a subarea node as it has in the past, but it has additional capabilities. A basic example is that it can appear to other APPN nodes as an APPN node also.

The net effect of this is the integration of APPN nodes into subarea nodes with operational transparency. There is also less system definitions required, resources can be located dynamically, and route selection is dynamic.

VTAM V.4 R.1 Node Support

VTAM can perform different types of roles in respect to nodes with the addition of APPN support. These features/functions supported include:

1. *Interchange Node* When VTAM performs the role of an interchange node it is capable of providing the following functions:

   • Network Node. To an APPN network, VTAM appears to be an NN.
   • Subarea Node. To traditional SNA networks it is capable of performing cross domain resource manager functions, and it can perform other functions usually provided prior to the Version 4 Release 1 edition.

2. *Migration Data Host* If VTAM performs this type role it is probably not maintaining many (if any) subarea connections. In this capacity, VTAM's focus is application processing. It does still have the ability to control resources considered local. According to IBM, in this capacity VTAM would seem like a LEN End Node to an APPN environment, and it would appear like a subarea node in the traditional sense. Consequently, it is capable of performing with APPN nodes as well as subarea nodes. In this capacity VTAM has the capability to perform peer functions and still perform traditional VTAM functions as well.

3. *Subarea Node* This is how VTAM appeared prior to Version 4 Release 1. In this arrangement, VTAM was the center of the network, if you will. It can still do this in Version 4 Release 1.

4. *End Node* As an end node VTAM operates as follows:

   • Communicates with its designated network node server.
   • Cannot function with an NCP as in the traditional sense of ownership, nor can it provide activation/deactivation abilities for it.
   • Can be attached to other LEN or APPN End Nodes.
   • Must be connected to at least one network node server.

5. *Network Node* VTAM can function as an APPN network node. When operating as such its capabilities and limitations include:

   • Routing functions
   • Cannot own an NCP in the traditional sense
   • Cannot support subarea connections
   • Permits queries by other network nodes
   • Performs searches for unknown resource locations

Much more could be said about the APPN support with VTAM Version 4 Release 1, but this information provides the basics of the relationship between VTAM and APPN.

6.4   Type 2.1 End Node Architecture

As stated previously, APPN delineates three types of nodes:

- Network Node (NN)
- APPN End Node
- LEN End Node

Both kinds of end nodes have components in common. A list of those components include:

1) A Data Link Control Component

2) A Path Control Component

3) Logical Units

4) A Control Point

5) Application Transaction Programs

6) A Node Operator Facility

Figure 6.2 depicts conceptually how these components are structured.

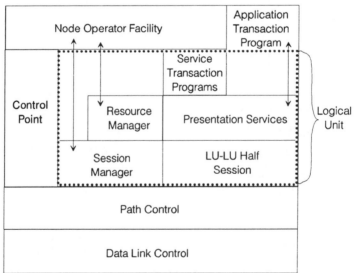

Figure 6.2   Type 2.1 APPN or LEN Node Structure

Using figure 6.2 as a reference, consider the following explanations of each component.

Data Link Control (DLC)   This component's name implies what it does; that is control the data link between two nodes. It is responsible for delivery of reliable information passed between nodes. This component has two parts:

1) Manager. This part of the DLC is responsible for link activation/deactivation. It manages data being passed to and from the Control Point (CP). And, it activates/deactivates the element.

2) Element. It interacts with the physical link connection. It also is that part of the DLC that performs retransmissions when required. It literally passes data to the physical media.

Path Control (PC)   Path control has a manager and element also. The manager performs session connection/termination. It also removes any data residing in queues once a session is terminated gracefully. The element routes messages CP and LU half sessions. It also performs error checking and performs prioritization if used.

Logical Units (LUs)   LUs are an entry point into the network. Figure 6.3 is an example of how its components appear.

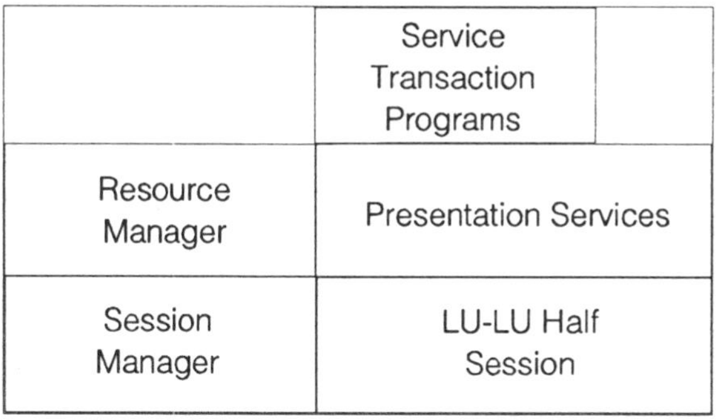

	Service Transaction Programs	
Resource Manager	Presentation Services	
Session Manager	LU-LU Half Session	

Figure 6.3   Logical Unit Structure in Type 2.1 Nodes

LU structure in this node includes the following functioning components:

1. Half Session. This controls communication between LUs at a session level. It actually performs data flow control and transmission control. An example of data flow control functions would be building and insuring proper parameters are used. An example of transmission control would be provision of session level pacing.

2. Session Manager. This sends and receives the BIND. (This type BIND consists of the same information as the BIND mentioned previously in this book.) It also manages session initiation with the control point.

3. Presentation Services. This part manages transaction programs and conversations between them. Functionally, it maintains the send/receive state between transaction programs.

4. Resource Manager. It is above presentation services in the sense it manages it. The resource manager has the ability to create and terminate presentation service support. It performs a critical role by verifying session level security. It checks passwords and controls access to transaction programs.

5. Service Transaction Programs. These are programs that actually make up the transaction services layer of SNA. A function named Change Number of Sessions (CNOS) is supported here. CNOS permits regulation of parallel sessions in the sense of activation/deactivation.

Control Point (CP)   This is the node manager. It communicates with other CPs in the network and exchanges pertinent information when required. In some respects, it is similar to the SSCP in VTAM found in subarea networks.

Application Transaction Programs   These are programs that utilize the resources available to them via the service transaction program component of the LU mentioned previously. They are typically custom written applications.

Node Operator Facility   The node operator facility performs many functions. It is the interface the node operator uses. A brief listing of functions it performs include:

- Node initialization
- Enables system (node) definition including:
  - session limits
  - node characteristics
  - link definition
  - other nodes it can communicate with
  - transaction program information
  - and other information
- Used to define LUs
- Used to activate/deactivate links
- Used to activate other node resources
- Used to start transaction programs
- And used for other functions

This is a brief synopsis of Type 2.1 end node architecture. For more information this author recommends referring to IBM's manual entitled, "Type 2.1 Node Reference." The IBM document number is SC30-3422.

6.5 Common Terms Used with APPN

APPN has terms that can be confusing to say the least. This section provides some terms commonly used in APPN discussions.

Address Space Reference to a set of addresses used for multiple functions. For example, an address space can identify sessions, links within a node, and adjacent link stations. Each Type 2.1 node has an address space for routing and for a transmission group whereby it can send messages.

Address Space Manager A component in Type 2.1 nodes that assigns and frees session addresses, thus occupying space.

Adjacent Node A term referring to a generic node that is logically or physically attached.

APPN End Node A Type 2.1 node capable of supporting sessions between its control point and a control point in an adjacent network node. It can be attached to multiple network nodes, but can only communicate with one network node's CP at a time. It selects a network node to be its server. It dynamically registers its LUs with its network node server. It also has the capability to support parallel links to other APPN nodes in an APPN network.

APPN Network Node   Also referred to as NN. It is a Type 2.1 node. It is capable of providing complete SNA end user services. It can also perform routing services within a Type 2.1 network. It provides its local LUs with required services and to attached end nodes in its domain. It also has the unique ability to function in a subarea network as a peripheral node.

APPN Intermediate Routing   Referencing the capability of an NN to route traffic from one node to another with the capability to control traffic flow.

Basic Information Unit (BIU)   Data and control information passed between half-sessions.

Basic Link Unit (BLU)   Data and control information transmitted over a link.

Basic Transmission Unit (BTU)   Data and control information sent back and forth between path control components.

Boundary Function   A component that has the capability to provide the following functions:

- Support attached peripheral node protocols
- Provide session level pacing
- Connect subarea path control and peripheral path control

Broadcast Search   The broadcast of a resource to all network nodes in an APPN network when the location of such resource is unknown.

Connection Network   The representation of a network transport facility shared within an APPN network.

Contention   A situation in a network where two NAUs (namely LUs) attempt to initiate the same action at the same time. For example, two LUs attempting to establish a session with one another simultaneously. In this scenario a contention winner and a contention loser is defined in order to break a deadlock situation.

Control Point   The component in a node that manages resources within that node. Depending upon the node type, it may provide services to other nodes.

Dependent Logical Unit (DLU)   A type of logical unit requiring an SSCP for LU-LU session establishment.

Directory   In APPN nodes, this is a listing, naming resources such as LUs and where they are located in the network.

Directory Services   That component of an APPN node that manages the directory and searches therein.

Distributed Directory Database   A full and complete listing of all resources in an APPN network as they are maintained in individual directories throughout an APPN network. This type implementation is where each node has a piece of the directory.

Flow Control   A process of managing the rate of data transfer between Type 2.1 nodes in an APPN network.

Half-Session   A component existing at the session layer that consists of data flow control and transmission control components at the end of a session.

Independent Logical Unit (ILU)   A type LU that does not require an SSCP to establish a session and then manage it. For example, LU6.2 is an ILU.

Intermediate Network Node   A node existing between the origin node and destination node within an APPN network and does not serve as a network file server for either originating or receiving node.

Intermediate Session Routing (ISR)   A routing function in an APPN network node providing session-level outage reporting and flow control for routes passing through this type node.

LEN End Node   A Type 2.1 node that can attach to other Type 2.1 nodes and use peer protocols. This type node can also attach to a subarea node as a peripheral node. It is capable of providing end user services to its LUs.

Link   A medium connecting two or more nodes.

Multiple Domain Network   In an APPN network a condition where more than one network node exists.

Network Node Server   A network node that provides services to its LUs and other nodes in the APPN network.

OLU   Origin Logical Unit.

Parallel Session Two or more logical connections that are concurrently active between the same two network accessible units but using different pairs of network addresses.

Path Control That function in APPN that provides paths between NAUs and routes messages between them.

Peripheral Node Typically a PU2.0 node; however, it can be a T2.1 node. If it is a PU2.0 node, it requires an SSCP to communicate with other nodes.

Route Selection Service A facility in Type 2.1 nodes that determines the best route for data traffic given a particular class of service.

Session A logical connection between two Network Accessible Units (NAUs).

Session Level Pacing A technique used to prevent a receiving LU from data overload during transmission.

Subarea A part of an SNA network that consists of any subarea nodes (such as processors) and any attached peripheral nodes including their resources.

System Services Control Point (SSCP) A component in a hierarchical network that controls PUs and LUs in its domain.

Topology Database A representation of the current network topology reflecting the intermediate routing in an APPN network.

Transaction Program An application transaction program is a customized program written by a user to perform a specific function; it uses LU6.2. A service transaction program is an IBM supplied transaction program operating in a node.

Transmission Group A collection of links between nodes.

Transport Network Synonymous with the path control network.

6.6 Conclusion

The appropriate conclusion to this chapter is to inform you this is but the tip of the iceberg of APPN and VTAM. Both have numerous books written in their name by IBM. This chapter has clarified APPN nodes by explaining their abilities and limitations. A brief examination presented advantages to Type 2.1 nodes. IBM's VTAM Version 4 Release 1 supports APPN functionality, and some of those aspects were presented so you will have a better understanding of VTAM's evolving role. Type 2.1 node architecture was presented briefly, just to show the robustness in the architecture. Some common APPN terms were presented because of the frequency they are used in APPN discussions.

Acronyms/Abbreviations

ABM	Asynchronous Balanced Mode
ABME	Asynchronous Balanced Mode Extended
ACB	Access Control Block
ACF/NCP	Advanced Communications Function for the Network Control Program
ACF/SSP	Advanced Communications Function for the System Support Program
ACF/VTAM	Advanced Communications Function for the Virtual Telecommunications Access Method
ACK	Positive Acknowledgement
ACT	Activate
ACTLINK	Activate Link
ACTLU	Activate Logical Unit
ACTPU	Activate Physical Unit
AID	Attention Identifier
ALT	Alternate
ANSI	American National Standard Institute
APA	All-Points-Addressable
APAR	Authorized Program Analysis Report
API	Application Programming Interface
APPC	Advanced Program-to-Program Communication
APPN	Advanced Peer-to-Peer Networking
APPL	Application
ASCII	American National Standard Code for Information Interchange
ASM	Address Space Manager
ASN.1	Abstract Syntax Notation One
ASYNC	Asynchronous
ATTN	Attention
B	Busy
BB	Begin Bracket
BBI	Begin Bracket Indicator
BC	Begin Chain

BCI	Begin Chain Indicator
BETB	Between-Bracket state
BF	Boundary Function
BIND	SNA BIND command
BIU	Basic Information Unit
BLU	Basic Link Unit
Bps	Bits Per Second
BSC	Binary Synchronous Communication
BTU	Basic Transmission Unit
BUFFSZ	Buffer Size
CAW	Channel Address Word
CBA	Current Buffer Address
CCITT	International Telegraph and Telephone Consultative Committee
CCW	Channel Command Word
CD	Cross Domain
CD	Change Direction
CDRM	Cross Domain Resource Manager
CE	Channel End
CEB	Conditional End of Bracket
CEBI	Conditional End of Bracket Indicator
CICS	Customer Information Control Systems
CID	Connection Identifier
CINIT	Control Initiate
CLAW	Common Link Access to Workstation
CLIST	Command List
CMS	Conversational Monitoring System
CNCL	Cancel
CNM	Communciation Network Management
CNOS	Change Number of Sessions
COMM	Communications
CONT	Contention
COS	Class of Service
CP	Control Point
CPI	Common Programming Interface

CPS	Characters Per Second
CPU	Central Processing Unit
CR	Command Reject
CR	Carriage Return
CSW	Channel Status Word
CTS	Clear to Send
CU	Control Unit
CUA	Common User Access
CUE	Control Unit End
CUT	Control Unit Terminal
CV	Control Vector
D	Display
DAF	Destination Address Field
DACTLU	Deactivate Logical Unit
DACTPU	Deactivate Physical Unit
DAF	Destination Address Field
DB	Device Busy
DBCS	Double Byte Character Set
DCA	Document Content Architecture
DCB	Device Control Block
DCE	Data-Circuit Terminating Equipment
DCE	Distributed Computing Environment
DCP	Destination Control Point
DEL	Delete
DEV	Device
DFC	Data Flow Control
DFS	Distributed File Service
DFSORT	Data Facility Sort
DIA	Document Interchange Architecture
DISC	Disconnect
DISOSS	Distributed Office System Support
DLC	Data Link Control
DLE	Data Link Escape
DLU	Dependent Logical Unit
DM	Disconnect Mode

DME	Distributed Management Environment
DR	Definite Response
DS	Directory Services
DSAP	Destination Service Access Point
DSR	Data Set Ready
DTE	Data Terminal Equipment
EAB	Extended Attribute Buffer
EB	End Bracket
EBCDIC	Extended Binary Coded Decimal Interchange Code
EC	End Chain
ECI	End of Chain Indicator
EIA	Electronic Industry Association
EM	End of Message
EN	End Node
ENQ	Enquiry
EOF	End of Field
EOR	End of Record
EOT	End of Transmission
ER	Explicit Route
ERI	Exception Response Indicator
ERP	Error Recovery Procedure
ESA	Enterprise System Architecture
ESC	Escape
ESCON	Enterprise System Connectivity
ETB	End of Transmission Block
ETX	End of Text
EX	Exception Response
EXR	Exception Request
FAP	Format and Protocol
FCS	Frame Check Sequence
FBA	Fixed Block Architecture
FDDI	Fiber Distributed Data Interface
FEP	Front End Processor
FF	Flip-Flop Direction Control
FF	Forms Feed

FID	Format Identifier
FIFO	First In First Out
FM	Function Management
FMH	Function Management Header
FMP	Function Management Profile
FRMR	Frame Reject Response
FSM	Finite State Machine
GCS	Group Control System
GDDM	Graphical Data Display Manager
GDS	General Data Stream
GE	Graphic Escape
GP	General Poll
GOSIP	Government Open Systems Interconnection Profile
GTF	Generalized Trace Facility
HDX	Half Duplex Data Flow
HS	Half Session
HSCB	Half Session Control Block
HDLC	High Level Data Link Control Protocol
Hex	Hexadecimal
HT	Horizontal Tab
Hz	Hertz
I	Information
IBM	International Business Machines
ID	Indentification
ID	Identifier
IEEE	Institute of Electrical and Electronic Engineers
IML	Initial Machine Load (initial microprogram load)
ILU	Independent Logical Unit
INB	In Bracket State
INN	Intermediate Network Node
INS	Insert
I/O	Input/Output
IOS	Input/Output Supervisor
IPCS	Interactive Problem Control System
IPDS	Intelligent Printer Data Stream

IPL	Initial Program Load
ISO	International Standard Organization
ISPF	Interactive System Product Facility
ISR	Intermediate Session Routing
ITSC	International Technical Support Center
IUCV	Inter-User Communication Vehicle
JCL	Job Control Language
k	1000
K	1024
KANA	Katakana
KB	KiloByte
KBD	Keyboard
LAN	Local Area Network
LC	Logical Channel
LCID	Logical Channel Identifier
LEN	Low Entry Networking
LF	Line Feed
LH	Link Header
LIC	Last in Chain
LLC	Logical Link Control
LU	Logical Unit
LUSTAT	LU Status
MB	MegaByte
MAC	Media Access Control
MAN	Metropolitan Area Network
MU	Message Unit
MVS	Multiple Virtual Storage
MVS/ESA	Multiple Virtual Storage Enterprise System Architecture
MVS/SP	Multiple Virtual Storage System Product
MVS/XA	Multiple Virtual Storage Extended Architecture
NA	Network Address
NAU	Network Accessible Unit
NACK	Negative Acknowledgement
NCCF	Network Communication Command Facility

NCP	Network Control Program
NETBIOS	Network Basic Input Output System
NFS	Network File System
NIC	Network Interface Card
NMVT	Network Management Vector Transport
NN	Network Node
NNS	Network Node Server
NOP	No Operation
NORM	Normal Flow
NPSI	Network Packet Switched Interface
NPDA	Network Problem Determination Application
NRZ	Non-Return-to-Zero
NS	Network Services
NSAP	Network Service Access Point
NTO	Network Terminal Option
NVT	Network Virtual Terminal
OAF	Origin Address Field
OC	Operation Check
OV/MVS	Office Vision/Multiple Virtual Storage
P	Primary
PA	Program Access
PC	Path Control
PC	Personal Computer
PI	Pacing Indicator
PIU	Path Information Unit
PLU	Primary Logical Unit
PRI	Primary
PROFS	Professional Office System
PRTY	Priority
PS	Present Services
PSWD	Password
PTF	Program Temporary Fix
PU	Physical Unit
PUCP	Physical Unit Control Point

PUT	Program Update Tape
PVC	Permanent Virtual Circuit
Q	Queue
QC	Quiesce Complete
QLLC	Qualified Link Control
QR	Queued Response
QRI	Queued Response Indicator
RACF	Resource Access Control Program
RB	Read Buffer
RCD	Request Change Direction
RCV	Receive
RD	Request Disconnect
REC	Receive
RNR	Receive Not Ready
RESP	Response
RH	Request or Response Header
RJE	Remote Job Entry
RR	Receive Ready
R/R	Request or Response
RSCS	Remote Spooling Communications Subsystem
RSHUTD	Request Shutdown
RSP	Response
RSS	Route Selection Services
RST	Reset
RTM	Response Time Monitor
RTS	Request to Send
RU	Request or Response Unit
S	Secondary
SA	Set Attribute
SAA	System Application Architecture
SABM	Set Asynchronous Balanced Mode
SABME	Set Asynchronous Balanced Mode Extended
SAP	Service Access Point
SARM	Set Asynchronous Response Mode
SBA	Set Buffer Address

SC	Session Control
SCS	SNA Character String
SDLC	Synchronous Data Link Communication
SDT	Start Data Traffic
SESS	Session
SF	Start Field
SHUTC	Shutdown complete
SHUTD	Shutdown
SIT	System Initialization Table
SLU	Secondary Logical Unit
SM	Session Manager
SMP/E	System Modification Program Extended
SNA	Systems Network Architecture
SNADS	SNA Distribution Services
SNI	SNA Network Interconnection
SNRM	Set Normal Response Mode
SP	System Product
SS	Session Services
SSAP	Source Service Access Point
SSCP	System Services Control Point
STX	Start of Text
SUW	Synchronized Unit of Work
SVC	Services
SYNC	Synchronization
T2	Type 2.0 Node
T2.1	Type 2.1 Node
T4	Type 4 Node
T5	Type 5 Node
TAF	Target Access Field
TCB	Transmission Control Block
TCT	Terminal Control Table
TCU	Transmission Control Unit
TDM	Topology Database Manager
TDU	Topology Database Update

TERM	Terminate
TG	Transmission Group
TH	Transmission Header
TPF	Transmission Priority
TS	Transmission Services
TSO	Time Sharing Option
U	Unprotected
UA	Unnumbered Acknowledgement
UI	Unnumbered Information
ULP	Upper Layer Protocol
VM	Virtual Machine
VM/ESA	Virtual Machine Enterprise System Architecture
VM/SP	Virtual Machine System Product
VM/XA	Virtual Machine Extended Architecture
VR	Virtual Route
VSE	Virtual Storage Extended
VTAM	Vitual Telecommunication Access Method
VTOC	Volume Table of Contents
WCC	Write Control Character
WAN	Wide Area Network
WSF	Write Structured Field
X	X Window System
XA	Extended Architecture
XID	Exchange Identifier
ZPAR	Zero Partitions

Glossary

Abstract Syntax Notation One (ASN.1)—A language used in OSI and TCP/IP networks to define datatypes for use in network management.

Access Method—Software residing in large IBM processors that perform multiple tasks in the network. A fundamental function it performs in a hierarchical network is aid in session establishment. It also serves as a controlling point in an SNA network. It performs other functions as well.

Adjacent Nodes—Nodes connected by one or more links with no nodes between them.

ACTLU—Activate Logical Unit. An SNA command issued to start a session on a logical unit.

ACTPU—Activate Physical Unit. An SNA command issued to start a session on a physical unit.

Address—An identifiable location. A location within memory. A location of a node within a network. A reference to a particular point with a computer or network environment. A way of identifying a network, subnetwork, or node.

Advanced Peer-to-Peer Networking (APPN)—Technically, it is an extension to SNA. It is peer based; this is in contrast to hierarchical based SNA. The forte of APPN is routing.

APPN End Node—A Type 2.1 node supporting sessions between its control point and the control point in an adjacent network node. This type node can also function as a peripheral node in a subarea.

APPN Network Node—A T2.1 node that offers end user services, routing functions, and network services to local LUs and also attached end nodes in its domain

Advanced Program-to-Program Communication (APPC)—Data communication at a peer level based on LU6.2 protocols.

Address Space—An identified range of addresses available to an application program.

AID key—Attention Identifier Key. A 3270 key that contains a specific code in the inbound 3270 data stream that identifies the source or type of data that follows. A character in the data stream that indicates a user has pressed a key that requires action by the system; examples of AID keys include: ENTER, Print, Page Up, Page Down, and Home keys.

API—Application Program Interface. Defined routines that are callable services by a program.

Alert—A message that can be sent to a management focal point (such as NetView) providing status information about a node.

Application Layer—The topmost layer in the OSI reference model that aids in the identification of communicating partners. It performs the following functions: establishes the authority to communicate; supports file services, electronic mail, print services; and transfers information.

ASCII—American National Standard Code for Information Interchange. ASCII is a character set defining alphanumeric characters. 128 possible binary arrangements exist.

Asynchronous—Also called async. Without a regular time relationship.

Boundary Function—An ability of a subarea node to provide services to peripheral nodes such as protocol support, transform network addresses. This function is provided by a component in a subarea node.

Backbone—A term used to refer to a set of nodes and links that are connected and together comprise the core components of a network.

Bandwidth—Refers to the range of frequencies transmitted on a channel. The difference between the highest and lowest frequencies transmitted across a channel.

Basic Conversation—A temporary connection between application programs in APPC. It is also an APPC session where the user must provide all information on how data is formatted.

Baud—The number of times per second a signal can change states on a transmission line.

BER—Bit Error Rate.

BIND—In SNA it is a command to activate a session between two logical units.

BIND Image—Session parameters passed in a control initiate (CINIT) request from the SSCP to the primary logical unit.

Bit rate—The rate, typically expressed in seconds, that bits are transmitted.

Block Mode—A string of data recorded or transmitted as a unit. Block mode transmission is the normal transmission mode in an SNA environment.

Bridge—A network device capable of connecting networks using similar protocols.

Broadband—A range of frequencies divided into narrow "bands" each of which can be used for different transmission purposes. Also known as wideband.

Broadband signaling—A type of signaling used in Local Area Networks that use analog signals, implement carrier frequencies, and multiplex more than one transmission at a given instance in time.

Broadcast—Simultaneous transmission of the same data to all nodes connected to the same medium.

Brouter—A network device capable of performing the function of a bridge while simultaneously filtering protocols and/or packets destined for nodes on a different network.

Burst Mode—A transmission mode where data is transmitted in bursts rather than continuous streams.

BUS—A linear configuration with respect to network topology.

Cache—An implementation of memory that usually operates faster than core or main memory. It is used to speed data and/or instruction transfer because it is designed to store frequently used data and/or instructions.

CICS—Customer Information Control System. An IBM licensed program offering enabling transactions entered at physically remote locations to be processed concurrently, in real time. It has built into it the capability of building, maintaining, and using databases.

Class-of-Service—A provision in SNA that defines transmission priority, path security, and bandwidth.

Client/Server Architecture—A general phrase used to refer to a distributed application environment where a program exists that can initiate a session and a program exists to answer the requests of a client. The origin of this concept is most strongly rooted in the TCP/IP protocols.

Client/Server—Terms used to refer to a peer-to-peer method of operation of applications within hosts. Beyond this definition, it is used to convey different thoughts; usually a vendor defines its meaning, making the word nebulous.

Cluster Controller—An SNA device to which terminals and printers attach. Typically, this is a PU Type 2.0 node.

CMS—Conversational Monitoring System. A component of VM operating system providing interactive time sharing, program development capabilities, and a mechanism for problem solving. CMS operates under the control of the VM Control Program (CP).

Command Facility—A component of NetView which is the base for command processors that can monitor, control, and automate the SNA network.

Control Program (CP)—A component of VM that manages resources such as CMS and components of a single machine so that the appearance of multiple computers is possible.

CNM—Communication Network Management. Managing the distribution of information and control among users of communication systems.

CNM application—IBM's NetView program. An application that interacts with PUs from a network management aspect.

CNM interface—That point of common ground which an access method has with an application program.

Compile—To translate a program written in a high-level language into machine language. Thus the program is executable.

Communication Controller Node—A device that contains a Network Control Program (NCP). This type node manages links and routing of data throughout the network.

Connection—A link between two or more entities. Connections may be logical or physical.

Contention—A scenario where two NAUs attempt to initiate the same action, at the same time. To eliminate the possibility of this happening, LUs are defined as contention winners and contention losers.

Contention Loser—An NAU defined to function as a loser in a state of contention.

Contention Winner—An NAU defined to function as a winner in a state of contention.

Control Point (CP)—Tasks that provide directory and routing functions for advanced peer-to-peer networking (APPN) nodes. A control point provides session and routing services.

Control Unit Terminal (CUT)—A type of protocol used by a 3174 or its predecessor, the 3274, where the controller interprets the data stream. Some terminals that rely on this type data stream include the following: 3178, 3179, 3278 model 2, and a 3279 model S2A. CUT terminals keep screen modifications or whatever operator changes made locally in a buffer until an Attention Identifier key is pressed or the Enter key is pressed, thus passing the buffered data upstream.

Conversation—The communication between two transaction programs using LU6.2 protocols through a logical unit (LU).

CP-to-CP Session—A logical connection (session) between two controlling points, typically in supporting APPN nodes. This session uses LU6.2 protocols. The session is used to exchange required management and other related information.

Cross Domain—A particular term used in SNA referring to the control of resources in more than one domain.

Crosstalk—A term referring to signals that interfered with another signal being transmitted.

CUT mode—An interactive host mode permitting an IBM 3270 personal computer (that has been customized for this mode) to use a session emulating a terminal type used in CUT mode.

DACTLU—Deactivate Logical Unit. An SNA command used to end one or more sessions on a physical unit (PU).

DACTPU—Deactivate Physical Unit. An SNA command used to end a session with a physical unit.

Data—A generic reference to alphanumeric characters within a computer or related device.

Data flow control layer—In SNA, that layer where data flow is regulated between half sessions.

Data link—The part of a node that is controlled by a data link protocol. It is the logical connection between two nodes.

Data link protocol—A prescribed way of handling the establishment, maintenance, and termination of a logical link between nodes. Examples of data link protocols include: Token Ring, SDLC, channel, etc.

Data set—This is how data, programs, etc. are stored in the MVS operating system. Different types of data sets exist; for example, partitioned data sets and sequential data sets.

Data stream—All data and control information sent across a link. In SNA different type data streams include 3270 data stream, 5250 data stream, and SNA Character String.

DB2—Data Base 2. IBM's licensed data base program which operates under certain operating systems.

Deactivate—An SNA term used to refer to the action taken to remove a device from the state of active.

Dependent Logical Unit (DLU)—Any logical unit (LU) that requires an SSCP to aid in establishing a LU-LU session. This type LU receives the SNA ACTLU command over a defined link. Also referred to as an SSCP dependent LU.

Destination—A point or location to which data is to be sent.

DIA—In SNA, Document Interchange Architecture. This defines protocols for the exchange of information between office applications.

Digital—Referring to a state of on or off; representing a binary 1 or a binary 0.

Directory Services—A component in an APPN node that maintains a directory of nodes in the network and manages the searches in the directory.

Distributed Computing Environment (DCE)—An Open Software Foundation (OSF) defined set of technologies supporting distributed computing environments.

Distributed File Service—An Open Software Foundation (OSF) file server technology.

Distributed Management Environment—An Open Software Foundation (OSF) system and network management technology.

Distributed Processing—The act of processing storage, I/O processing, control functions, and actual processing is dispersed among two or more nodes.

Domain—A defined area in SNA where resources reside under a common control. Some resources referred to here include: SSCPs, PUs, LUs, links, link stations, etc.

Domain Name—In a TCP/IP network, a name associated to a host system in a network.

Double Byte Character Set—A character set where alphanumeric characters are represented by two bytes. Examples of languages where this is used include: Japanese, Chinese, and Korean.

Downstream—In SNA, this refers to the direction of data flow. Typically, a host is considered the top of the "stream" and other nodes are downstream from there.

Dynamic Definition of LUs—VTAM's ability to dynamically create a definition of an LU after receiving a session initiation request from a particular LU.

Dynamic Link Library (DLL)—A programming module that contains dynamic link routines which are linked at load or execution time.

EBCDIC—Extended Binary Coded Decimal Interchange Code. IBM's character set used in SNA. This character set is the foundation where data streams such as 3270, etc. get their components, making up a particular data stream.

Emulation—To simulate the real thing.

3270 Emulation—An application program that emulates the functions and 3270 data stream, appearing as if it were a genuine 3270 data stream.

End Node (LEN)—In SNA, an APPN node that only has the capability of being a target or source node. It cannot perform any routing functions.

End User—Known in SNA as a person, application, device, or even a computer system that utilizes resources in a network.

Enterprise Network—Generally agreed to be a wide area network providing services to all corporate sites. In many instances it has a nebulous meaning, typically defined by the individual or vendor using the term.

Environmental Recording Editing and Printing Program (EREP)—A software package that makes data gathered and contained in a system file recorder available for analysis at a later date.

ESCD—Enterprise Systems Connection Director.

ESCD Console—Typically, a PS/2 used to perform operator functions and other tasks related to the ESCON director.

ESCM—ESCON manager.

ESCON—Enterprise Systems Connection. Collectively, it refers to IBM's product offerings that include hardware and software. Generally, the term is used to refer to IBM's fiber data channel.

ESCON Channel—A channel using fiber optic cabling as the transmission medium.

ESCON Director—A device used to control and provide connectivity capabilities between ESCON links.

ESCON Environment—A data processing environment using ESCON (fiber optic cabling) as the transmission medium.

ESCON Manager—An IBM licensed program providing host control and communication capabilities for ESCON director connections.

Event—An occurrence. For example, an occurrence significant to a specific task.

Exchange Identification (XID)—An id that is exchanged with a remote PU when an attachment is first made.

EXCP—Execute Channel Program.

Expanded Memory—Additional memory available to processors. It is typically as fast as internal memory or (RAM).

Explicit Route—In SNA, a set of two or more transmission groups that connect two subarea nodes.

Extended Memory—A word used frequently with the OS/2 operating system referring to memory beyond 1 MB.

Extended Storage—A word used in relation to the VM/SP High Performance Option (HPO) operating system. It is implemented in large processors and certain releases of the VM operating system. It is considered an extension to real storage that is accessed synchronously in 4Kbyte increments.

External Storage—Storage accessible to a processor only via I/O channels.

Extent—A term used in SNA to refer to a contiguous space on a disk or diskette that is occupied (or reserved) for a data set.

External Domain—A part of an SNA network that is controlled by an SSCP that is not part of that segment.

External Storage—Storage accessible to processors only via I/O channels, be they parallel or ESCON channels.

FDDI—Fiber Distributed Data Interface. An ANSI defined standard for high speed data transfer over fiber optic cabling.

Fixed Length Record—Those components that make up a file. In this case, all records have the same length as other records comprising the file.

Flow Control—That process which manages the rate data passes between components in an SNA network.

Focal Point—The control point in an SNA network which receives alerts.

Front end processor (FEP)—Used to refer to a communication controller node.

Frame—Typically, this term refers to data and all TCP/IP headers and trailers including ETHERNET. All this is referred to as a frame.

Frame Relay—A switching mechanism for routing frames as quickly as possible.

Gateway—When used with the Internet, traditionally this term referred to a device that performs a routing function. Now the term refers to a networking device that translates protocols of one type network into protocols of another type network.

Gateway Node—A device that is an interface between networks. IBM uses the term as synonymous for a gateway NCP.

GDDM—An IBM term meaning Graphical Data Display Manager.

Generalized Trace Facility—A program that can record significant system events like supervisor calls and start I/O operations, so problem determination can be achieved.

GTF Trace—See generalized trace facility.

Giga—It means 1,000,000,000 in decimal notation.

Gigabyte—One billion bytes. When written in decimal notation this means: 1,073,741,824.

Graphic Escape Character—A specific escape code in the 3270 data stream. It is used to introduce a graphic character from a different character set. The code is hexadecimal 80.

Graphic Primitive—A basic element, like an arc or line not made up of smaller parts.

Graphical Data Display Manager—A group of routines allowing drawings to be defined and displayed corresponding to graphic primitives.

GOSIP—Government Open System Interconnection Profile. This is a government standard using the OSI reference model.

Group Control System (GCS)—A part of the VM operating system that provides multiprogramming and memory sharing support to virtual machines.

GVM—Guest Virtual Machine.

Half Session—Within SNA, this is a component providing function management data, services, data flow control, and transmission control for a session in a network addressable unit.

Hierarchical Computer Network—A network where control functions are organized in a hierarchical manner. These functions can be distributed among nodes in the network.

High Function Terminal (HFT)—A type of terminal typically used with RISC/6000 machines and the AIX operating system.

High Level Data Link Control (HDLC)—An international data communication standard that specifies a particular order for a series of bits.

High Performance Option (HPO)—An extension program to VM/SP (system product—the base operating system). It provides operational enhancements for large systems.

Host Command Facility (HCF)—A feature available on large systems that enables a user on such a large system to use applications on other systems (like an AS/400) as if they were using remotely attached 5250 type displays.

Host Logical Unit—In SNA, this is a logical unit located in a host node. An example would be a VTAM application program.

Host node—In SNA, this is a node containing an SSCP and providing application service support.

Host processor—In SNA, a processor that controls applications in a network.

Host subarea—In SNA, a subarea that contains a processor.

Hot Site—A computer center that is fully capable of providing resources, duplicating a designated data center.

Hot Standby—A site maintained in complete readiness to manually switch over immediately in case of failure of the primary site.

Hot Swap—The automatic switch-over from a primary site to a hot site. This type swap requires NO human intervention. The swap is automatic.

Hung Terminal—Reference to a terminal that is apparently locked. In actuality, the LU used by the terminal is in a hung state. In such state, the terminal can neither send nor receive commands.

ICCF—Interactive Computing and Control Facility. Used in the VSE operating system.

IEEE—Institute of Electrical and Electronic Engineers.

IEEE 802.5—A standard defining the physical layer using a token passing technology implemented on a ring topology.

IMS—Information Management System. An IBM program offering that is a combination database and data communication system.

Inactive—In SNA, the state of a resource. It means that resource is not operational.

Independent Logical Unit—Technically defined as a logical unit that does not receive an SNA command (ACTLU) over a data link. This type LU can be either primary or secondary. It can also have multiple sessions occurring simultaneously.

Inhibit—A mode that 3270 terminals, and other devices, can get into thus not accepting any interruptions. A reset must be performed.

Initiate—A request sent from an LU to an SSCP requesting a LU-LU session.

Intelligent Printer Data Stream (IPDS)—This is an all-points-addressable data stream that permits data, images, or graphics at any defined point on the printed page.

Interactive Computing and Control Facility—A VSE operating system controlling computer system availability on a time sharing basis.

Interface—A shared point between two entities, be they software or hardware.

Interpreter—A program that takes high level language programs and translates them, one line at a time, into machine language. Typically, an interpreter is slower than a compiler because a compiled program is processed prior to execution time, whereas the interpreted program is converted into machine language in real time, immediately before execution.

Inter-User Communication Vehicle (IUCV)—A VM operating system facility used for passing data between virtual machines and VM components.

IOCP—Input/Output Control Program. A program used to define all devices connected to the I/O subsystem.

ISPF—Interactive System Product Facility. An IBM program offering that has full screen editing capabilities.

ISO Reference Model—The networking model created by the International Standard Organization defining seven layers of a network, isolating functions within each layer. It is used as a baseline for comparison/contrast of other network types.

ISTATUS—A VATM and NCP definition specification that indicates the initial status of resources.

IUCV—See Inter-user communication vehicle.

JCL—Job Control Language.

JES2—An MVS subsystem that serves as a waiting room prior to execution. JES2 converts jobs to an internal format and selects them for execution. JES2 is used in installations with more than one processor where each JES2 independently controls its job input, scheduling, and output.

JES3—A MVS subsystem that serves as a waiting room prior to execution. It is similar to JES2, but it differs in that JES3 manages processors in complexes that are loosely coupled and have several processors.

Job—A term used to refer to a unit of work. The unit of work is user defined and computer executed.

Job Control Language—A language used to define jobs to the operating system for execution. The language defines job requirements and other parameters.

Job Name—The way a job is identified to a system.

Job Priority—A value assigned to a job that reflects priority of execution, resources, etc.

Kilobyte—1024 bytes.

LAN—Local Area Network. A collection of computer related equipment connected in such a way that communication can occur between all nodes connected to the medium.

Learning Bridge—A special type network device. It serves the function of a bridge, but it has the capability to learn what nodes are connected and route data accordingly.

Leased Line—A dedicated communication line between two points. This type line is a constant vehicle for logical communications to occur at all times. Contrast this with switched line.

LEN—Low Entry Networking Node. A type of APPN node.

Link—A generic term used to refer to a connection between two end points.

Library—A file or set of related files. Loosely referred to as a partitioned data set. Sometimes a PARMLIB.

Line Speed—The rate at which data is transmitted from a designated point to another.

Lobe—A term used in token ring. Specifically, the attaching cable between the token ring interface board and the media access unit (MAU).

Local non-SNA major node—A channel attached major node that has non-SNA terminals attached.

Local SNA major node—A channel attached major node whose terminals are included and considered collectively as peripheral nodes.

Local workstation—A terminal directly connected to a system.

Logical—A generic term used to refer to convey an abstract meaning or implementation. It is typically the antithesis of Physical.

Logical Link Control (LLC)—The upper part of the data link sublayer protocol responsible for controlling exchange of data between two end points.

Logical Unit (LU)—In SNA, an end point.

Logical Unit Name—A name used to reflect the address of a logical unit (logical unit being defined as an addressable end point).

Logoff—The request by a user to terminate a session. Technically, it is a VTAM unformatted session termination request.

Logon—A request by a user to initiate a session (go into a LU-LU session). Technically, a session initiation request.

Logon Mode Table (LOGMODE)—An entry in the SYS1.VTAMLST data set that in turn includes entries reflecting particular types of LU session parameters.

Low Entry Networking—In SNA, a particular implementation of T2.1 architecture that permits peer communication between two nodes.

Low Entry Networking Node—LEN Node. A 2.1 architected node using LU6.2, but not capable of routing and other functions performed by a network node.

LU-LU session—A logical connection between two logical units.

MAC—Media Access Control. The lower half of the data link sublayer. It is responsible for framing data and controlling the physical link between two stations.

Mainframe—A general term, normally used to refer to IBM's largest hardware architected machines. For example, the 3090 and 4300 series machines would fit this category. The ES/9000 processor line would fit this category as well.

Management Services—A type of service provided by an SSCP on LUs. Some examples include the passing of a request for network data, reporting error statistics, etc.

Major node—In SNA, this is a set of VTAM resources which can be activated and/or deactivated as a single group.

Mapped Conversation—In APPC, a mechanism whereby the system provides information as to how data is formatted.

Medium Access Unit (MAU)—A device for central connection of nodes operating in a network.

Member—A part of a partitioned data set. It is similar to a file.

Menu—A list of choices presented in a preformatted pattern.

Microcode—IBM's term used to refer to firmware. It is a set of instructions inside a programmable read only memory chip.

Minor node—A uniquely defined node within a major node. A VTAM definition.

Modem—A device that converts digital signals into analog signals and vice versa.

Multiple-Domain Network—In SNA, a network with more than one host node, each containing an SSCP.

Multiple explicit routes—Two or more routes between subarea nodes.

Multiplex—To simultaneously transmit multiple signals over one channel.

Multipoint—Describing communication between two stations over a single telecommunication line.

Multiregion operation—A method of communication between CICS systems, within the same processor, not using SNA network facilities.

Multitailed—In SNA, a term used to refer to a communications controller node attached to more than one host.

MVS—IBM's Multiple Virtual Storage operating system.

Native mode—Referring to VTAM running directly on a VM operating system rather than on a guest operating system.

NCCF—Network Communications Control Facility. A part of IBM's NetView product offering used in network management.

NCP—Network Control Program. An IBM program operating on a communications controller node. It is software that performs routing and data flow control functions.

NCP major node—A set of minor nodes reflecting resources like lines and peripheral nodes, all controlled by the NCP.

Negotiable BIND—In SNA, the ability of two LUs to negotiate the session parameters once the session is activated.

NETBIOS—Network Basic Input Output Operating System. An IBM and compatible network programming interface.

NetView—IBM's software product offering used in management of SNA environments. NetView consists of software components such as Network Problem Determination Aid (NPDA), Network Logical Determination Manager (NLDM), and the Network Communications Control Facility (NCCF). NPDA is a hardware monitor. NLDM is a session monitor. NCCF is a command line providing support for various commands such as VTAM, etc.

Network—A collection of computers and related devices connected in such a way so that effective communication occurs.

Network Accessible Unit (NAU)—In SNA, this is an addressable point. Different types of NAUs include SSCPs, CPs, PUs, and LUs.

Network Interface Card (NIC)—A generic reference for a networking interface board.

Network Management—Reference to the control mechanism of a network. This may include monitoring, activation, and deactivation.

Network Management Vector Transport (NMVT)—An SNA management service request or response unit (RU) that is transmitted over an SSCP-PU session.

Node—A generic term used to refer to varying types of networking devices.

Node type—In SNA, nodes characterized by capabilities, function, PU architecture, or LU support.

Non-SNA—Meaning not a native SNA device.

Nonswappable—Referring to programs and/or data that must remain in storage.

Optical Fiber—Glass or plastic cable used as a communications medium.

Open Shortest Path First (OSPF)—An internet routing protocol that can route traffic via multiple paths using network topology. .

Open Systems Interconnection (OSI)—A set of ISO standards relating to data communications.

Operator Information Area—An SNA term referring to the 25th line on a 3270 terminal whereby symbols represent the status and state of the terminal with respect to the SNA environment.

Pacing—A function performed by a receiving station whereby it controls the rate of transmission of the sending station in order to prevent buffer overrun.

Page—A defined amount of data (fixed length) that is moved from internal to external storage during the function of virtual storage.

Paging—Moving part of a larger amount of data between internal and external storage.

Parallel Channel—IBM's name for a link that transmits data in parallel format. Contrast with ESCON.

Parallel link—Two or more links between subarea nodes.

Parallel session—Two or more concurrently active logical links between two LUs.

Partitioned Data Set (PDS)—A method used for storage under the MVS operating system. A PDS consists of a directory and members. The members in turn consist of records, which is the actual data.

Path—In SNA, this refers to a route from one point to another.

Path control—In traditional layered SNA, that part of the network which manages the sharing of link resources.

Path control network—That part of an SNA network that encompasses data link control and path control layers.

Peer—In SNA, a corresponding node.

Peer-to-Peer Communications—Reference to data communications between two nodes using LU6.2 sessions, whereby either node can initiate a conversation.

Peripheral link—A link that connects a peripheral node to a subarea node.

Peripheral logical unit—A logical unit in a peripheral node.

Peripheral node—In SNA, a network device that uses local addressing for routing rather than network addressing.

Physical control layer—In traditional SNA, that component providing the interface between the medium and the device to which the interface card is installed.

Physical Unit (PU)—Software implemented in such a way so that particular hardware takes on certain characteristics.

Physical Unit Control Point (PUCP)—A controlling component (portion) in the PU that functions in the activation of the PU and local related links.

Point-to-Point—Direct data transmission between two points without intervention from other devices in any way.

Point-to-Point Protocol (PPP)—This protocol has the ability to provide host-to-network and router-to-router connections over synchronous and asynchronous lines.

Polling—A function whereby stations attached on a multipoint or a point-to-point connection are asked to transmit data.

POSIX—Portable Operating System Interface For Computer Environment (POSIX). This is an IEEE standard for computer operating systems.

Presentation services layer—In traditional SNA, this is the layer that provides required services for transaction programs. It also controls conversation communication between them.

Primary Logical Unit—In SNA, the LU that initiates the SNA BIND command.

Processor—A central processing unit.

Protocol—A set of rules governing behavior or method of operation.

Protocol Conversion—Changing one type protocol (way of performing a task) to another type protocol (way of performing a task).

Quiesce—To end a process by permitting it to complete normal operations.

RACF—Resource Access Control Facility, IBM's security software product offering. RACF identifies and verifies users attempting to gain access to the system.

Remote device—Considered to be not in the same physical location as the processor (or target destination) with which it communicates.

Remote Job Entry (RJE)—The ability to submit jobs via terminal attached through some device in the SNA or non-SNA network.

Remote Spooling Communications Subsystem (RSCS)—An IBM software product that operates under the VM operating system. It supports command entry, provides spool file transfer capability, and messages between VM users.

Request/Response Unit—In SNA, a generic term used to refer to a request unit or a response unit.

Request Unit—In SNA, a message containing request or function management information.

Response Unit—In SNA, a message acknowledging a request unit.

Repeater—A network device that regenerates signals so the length of a network can be extended.

Resource—Generally used to refer to application programs, however it may be used in a general sense to refer to devices such as hardware. A resource can be referred to as being local, remote, network, or other characterizations.

Resource Access Control Facility (RACF)—An IBM licensed security package. It is used with MVS and verifies users, authorizing access to the system, and other security related functions.

Resource definition table—The main VTAM network configuration table; it is a table describing characteristics of all nodes available to VTAM programs. This table associates each node with a network address.

Response time—The amount of time between the end of an inquiry to the beginning of the response.

RISC/6000—IBM's line of processors and workstations that are based on RISC processors. They use the Advanced Interactive Executive (AIX) operating system, which is an implementation of UNIX.

Routine—A program, or part of a program, that serves a specific purpose; normally this purpose is calling another routine to perform a function.

Routing—A process of determining which path is to be used for data transmission.

RS-2332-C—A physical layer specification for connecting devices.

SAA—Systems Application Architecture. IBM's architecture, announced in March 1987, that defines a Common User Access (CUA), Common Programming Interface (CPI-C[using the C language]), and the Common Communications Support (CCS) components.

Same domain—Reference to communication between nodes within the same domain. Contrast with cross domain.

SAP—Service Access Point.

SDLC link—Communication of data over a link where control is maintained by synchronous data link control protocol (SDLC).

Secondary ESCON Manager—An ESCON manager whereby it receives a command from the primary ESCON manager via intersystem communication.

Secondary Logical Unit (SLU)—The requesting end of a dependent logical unit.

Selector Channel—An I/O channel architected to operate with only one I/O device at a time.

Serial—A description of events explaining that the occurrence of events is one after another. Contrast to parallel.

Session—In SNA, a logical connection between two end points. Different types of sessions exist and are required for SNA functions.

Session initiation request—An SNA initiate or logon request from an LU to an SSCP.

Session limit—According to the *IBM Dictionary of Computing*, "The maximum number of concurrently active LU-LU sessions an LU can support."

SNA—Systems Network Architecture. IBM's proprietary networking protocol announced in 1974. It is very prevalent worldwide and considered a reputable industry standard.

SNA Character String (SCS)—A particular data stream used in SNA consisting of EBCDIC control codes, end user data, and transported via a request/response unit.

SNA Distribution Services (SNADS)—An IBM set of rules defining asynchronous service for receiving, routing, and sending EMAIL in a multinetwork environment.

Source—The originating entity.

Subarea—In SNA, a part of a network that consists of attached peripheral nodes, associated resources, and as defined by SNA, a subarea node. Interestingly, no area nodes exist, only subarea nodes.

Subchannel—That part of a channel address identifying a particular device on a channel.

Subroutine—A set of instructions that are executed by a call from another program.

Swapping—A process that moves all program contents from internal to external storage and vice versa.

Switched connection—A data link connection that is similar to a telephone call. The link is established on demand. Thus reference to a switched line. Contrast a leased line.

Switched SNA major node—A PU and its associated LUs defined as a major node connected by switched links.

Synchronous Data Link Control (SDLC)—A code-transparent and serial, bit-by-bit data transfer over a physical link.

Synchronous Data Transfer—The physical transfer of data between two nodes that are clocked, or timed, and a predictable time relationship exists.

SYSGEN—The process of selecting and configuring parts of an operating system where the results are a customized operating system configured to meet specific site requirements.

System Services Control Point (SSCP)—In SNA, a focal point for managing the configuration and network resources. An SSCP exists in a host node, containing a PU 5.

Tera—A numeric quantity, when expressed in bytes, one terabyte is denoted as 1,009,511,627,766.

Terminate—An SNA request unit (RU) sent by an LU to an SSCP to start the procedure to end one or more LU-LU sessions.

Throughput—The amount of data that can be successfully moved across a medium or processed within a certain time period.

Time Sharing Option (TSO)—IBM's product offering that offers interactive development for users. It is actually a time sharing subsystem.

Token Ring—An IBM developed lower layer networking protocol using a token passing method controlling data traffic. It is connection oriented at a data link level.

Topology—The configuration of network devices. Examples include: BUS, Star, Ring, Dual Ring, etc.

Trace—A way by which execution of a program and the passing of data can be recorded for review.

Traffic—A generic term used to describe the amount of data on a network backbone at a given period in time.

Type 2.1 node—Any node that can function in SNA as a peripheral node using the protocols a Type 2.0 device utilizes. A Type 2.1 node using peer-to-peer protocols can connect directly to another Type 2.1 node.

UNBIND—In SNA, the command to deactivate a session between logical units.

Unformatted system services—An SSCP function that translates a user request into the appropriate format for system processing. For example, it takes a request to logon to an application and formats it such that required parameters can be applied to that session.

Unit of Work—In APPC it is an account of the amount of processing the source system starts, directly or indirectly.

Upstream—Referring to the opposite direction of data flow. Some use it to refer to the origin of transmission.

User—A person or program using system resources.

USS—Unformatted System Services.

Vary offline—In SNA, this means to put a resource in an inactive state.

Vary online—In SNA, this means to put a resource in an active state.

Virtual—Appearing to exist, but in reality the appearance is achieved by functions or processes.

Virtual Machine—An IBM operating system that supports operating systems running under its control.

Virtual Storage Extended (VSE)—An IBM operating system designed for users who need an S/390 or S/370 architected machine. It is best suited in small to intermediate data centers. It provides spooling, utilities, networking control, transaction processing, batch processing, and interactive processing as well as other functions.

Virtual Machine/System Product High Performance Option—An IBM software product that works with VM/SP. It provides enhancements to a VM/SP based machine.

Virtual route—A logical connection made over physical connections.

Virtual route pacing—Data flow control over virtual routes.

Virtual storage—That storage area referred to by an addressing scheme whereby real addresses are mapped to "unreal" addresses and vice versa.

Virtual Storage Extended (VSE)—An operating system. The product that followed DOS/VS. It is an operating system similar to MVS in that it is focused on production type environments. It performs control functions like other operating systems.

Virtual Telecommunications Access Method (VTAM)—Collectively, a set of programs that is the mediator between internal system resources (such as application subsystems and programs) and resources outside the system (such as disk drives and other devices). It is the dominant access method used today in 370/XA, ESA/370, and S/390 systems.

VM/SP directory—A CP disk file defining the configuration of a virtual machine. It includes user id, password, storage allocation, and so forth.

VM/370 Control Program (CP)—That component of a VM machine which manages resources of one computer and results in the appearance of multiple machines.

Volume—In SNA, this is another name given to a disk drive.

Volume Table of Contents (VTOC)—A directory of a disk drive's data sets.

VTAM definition—The identification of a program or other resource to VTAM.

Wide Area Network (WAN)—The term usually refers to a network spanning large geographic distances.

Workstation—This term connotes different meanings to different individuals. For example, it could be used to refer to a PC, an RISC based processor, or even a dumb terminal. At best its meaning is arbitrary.

X.400—A protocol defining standards for electronic mail in an open network.

X.500—A protocol defining standards for directory services in an open network.

Appendix A

MVS File Structure

This appendix is for users new to the MVS operating system. It provides basic information about file structures in an MVS environment.

MVS is a popular operating system in SNA. It stores data in a variety of ways. Data storage in MVS is called a data set. Multiple types of data sets exist, but two are commonly used by programmers and users alike.

The first type data set is called a partitioned data set (PDS); it is also referred to as a PARMLIB by some. Regardless the name, a PDS is similar to a directory with files. Figure 1 depicts a partitioned data set. Notice that records are located beside each member. Records are the data that is stored.

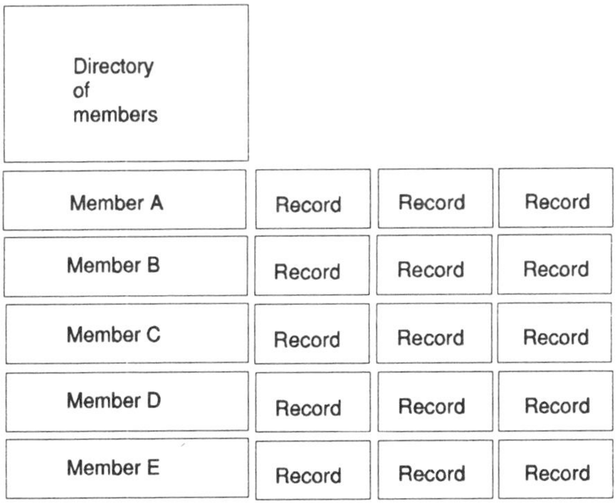

Directory of members			
Member A	Record	Record	Record
Member B	Record	Record	Record
Member C	Record	Record	Record
Member D	Record	Record	Record
Member E	Record	Record	Record

Figure 1   Partitioned Data Set

A second commonly used data set is known as a sequential data set. This is similar to a file. A sequential data set resides in a directory whose name is the same as the user logon id. Figure 2 is an example of a sequential data set.

Figure 2   Sequential Data Set

Notice beneath the sequential data set name are records. These records are data that comprise the data set.

In MVS data sets the concept of record formats exist. Three typical record formats and a brief description are:

- Fixed length. This means all records in a data set are the same length, in bytes. Consider figure 3 showing fixed length records.

Fixed Length Record Format

Record 1	Record 2	Record 3	Record 4

Figure 3   Fixed Format

- Variable length. These type records vary in length, some may be longer than others. Consider figure 4 showing variable length records.

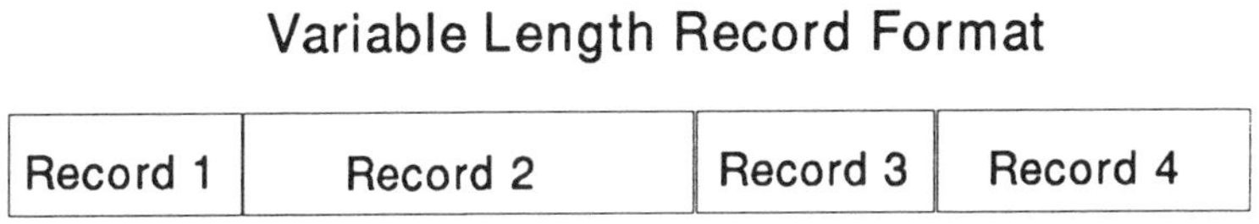

Variable Length Record Format

Record 1	Record 2	Record 3	Record 4

Figure 4   Variable Format

- Unspecified length. This type record has no prescribed length in terms of size. Consider figure 5 showing a record with an unspecified length.

Unspecified Length Record Format

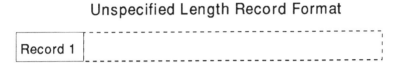

Figure 5   Unspecified Format

Other types of data sets exist in an MVS environment, but those are not the topic here. This appendix is a reference for users not familiar with partitioned or sequential data sets.

Appendix B

VM File Structure

This appendix is for users new to the VM operating system. It provides basic information about file structures in a VM environment. VM is also a popular operating system in SNA, used typically in development environments. It stores data differently than MVS, however.

System Directory

The VM operating system has been mentioned briefly, but additional information is needed here to aid in understanding data storage under VM. Each Guest operating system under VM "thinks" it is the only operating system in the machine. Each Guest operating system has access to only those physical system resources defined for it in the VM system directory. The system directory operates under CMS and is maintained by an operator with administrative privileges. Some administrative functions include: adding a directory for a newly defined user, changing the status of a user's capabilities, and/or changing a user's password. Other administrative functions include: generating a list of users, shutting down the system to perform maintenance, and other site dependent reasons.

Disks

Each physical VM disk (disks in the IBM world are also known as volumes) is partitioned into groups of tracks called minidisks. Each Conversational Monitoring System (CMS) disk volume has a master file directory containing names of all files on that physical disk. When a user accesses a particular minidisk the name(s) that person may access is paged into a user file directory residing in virtual storage. See figure 1.

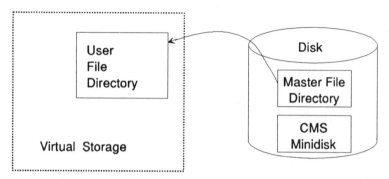

Figure 1   VM Disks

Consequently, a user thinks he/she has a minidisk, each with its own directory of filenames.

When a user updates a CMS file or creates a new file, information about this file is updated in the master file directory on the CMS disk volume and the user file directory in virtual storage.

Minidisks are available to CMS users in two modes: Read only and read/write. This applies to files, collectively, on a minidisk—not a file by file basis. For example, if a user has read only privileges, a file cannot be updated, but it can be browsed, copied, or executed. On the other hand, if a user has read/write privileges for a particular minidisk, each time the user updates a file, the user file and master file directory are updated immediately. Other users having read only access, to that particular minidisk, are not notified about the change(s).

Typically, CMS users are allowed read/write access to only one minidisk, called their "A" disk. All others are read only minidisks. Each minidisk is known by a letter, hence the maximum number of minidisks available to a user at one particular time is twenty six (26).

File Identification

A file is the fundamental unit of data in a CMS environment. Even though VM is a virtual machine supporting multiple preferred guest (MPG) operating systems, CMS disk files cannot be read or written to using other operating systems. CMS files are categorized by:

- Filename
- File type
- File mode

A filename is part of what gives CMS file its identity. Its uniqueness helps in the identification process. The filetype is a naming convention used to group files according to some common characteristic. For example, COBOL, ASSEMBLER, or EXECUTABLE. The filemode is an identifier consisting of two characters. First, the file mode indicates to CMS in which virtual minidisk the file resides. Second, the file mode is used to assign certain access characteristics to a file. For example, the number one (1) could represent a certain type file, whereas the number two (2) could represent another type file. Consider figure 2.

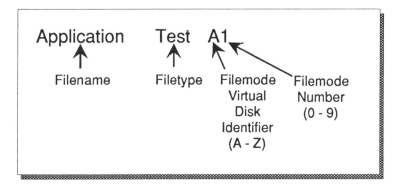

Figure 2   File Information

Records

The constituent parts of a file are records. Records can be fixed or variable length. In CMS, records constitute a line of data. If a file contains a fixed length record format, then it would appear as figure 3 shows.

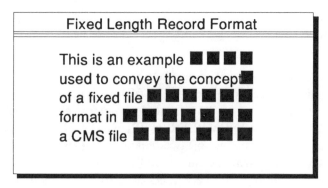

Fixed Length Record Format

This is an example ■ ■ ■ ■
used to convey the concept■
of a fixed file ■ ■ ■ ■ ■ ■
format in ■ ■ ■ ■ ■ ■ ■
a CMS file ■ ■ ■ ■ ■ ■

Figure 3   Fixed Format

Figure 3 shows a file where CMS fills trailing positions in a record with blanks. The advantage of this is fixed length records increase processing speeds; however, the disadvantage is disk space is not used efficiently.

Variable length records appear as figure 4 shows.

Variable Length Record Format

This is an example
used to convey
the
concept of a variable
file format
in
a CMS file

Figure 4   Variable Format

In variable length record format, CMS stores up to the last significant character only. In actuality, this amounts to less overhead than fixed length record format. However, the negative side of this format is processing time per record is increased.

VM file structure was architected around the VM operating system. Even though Multiple Preferred Guests (MPGs) can execute simultaneously on a VM machine, they each have their own file structures, respectively.

Index